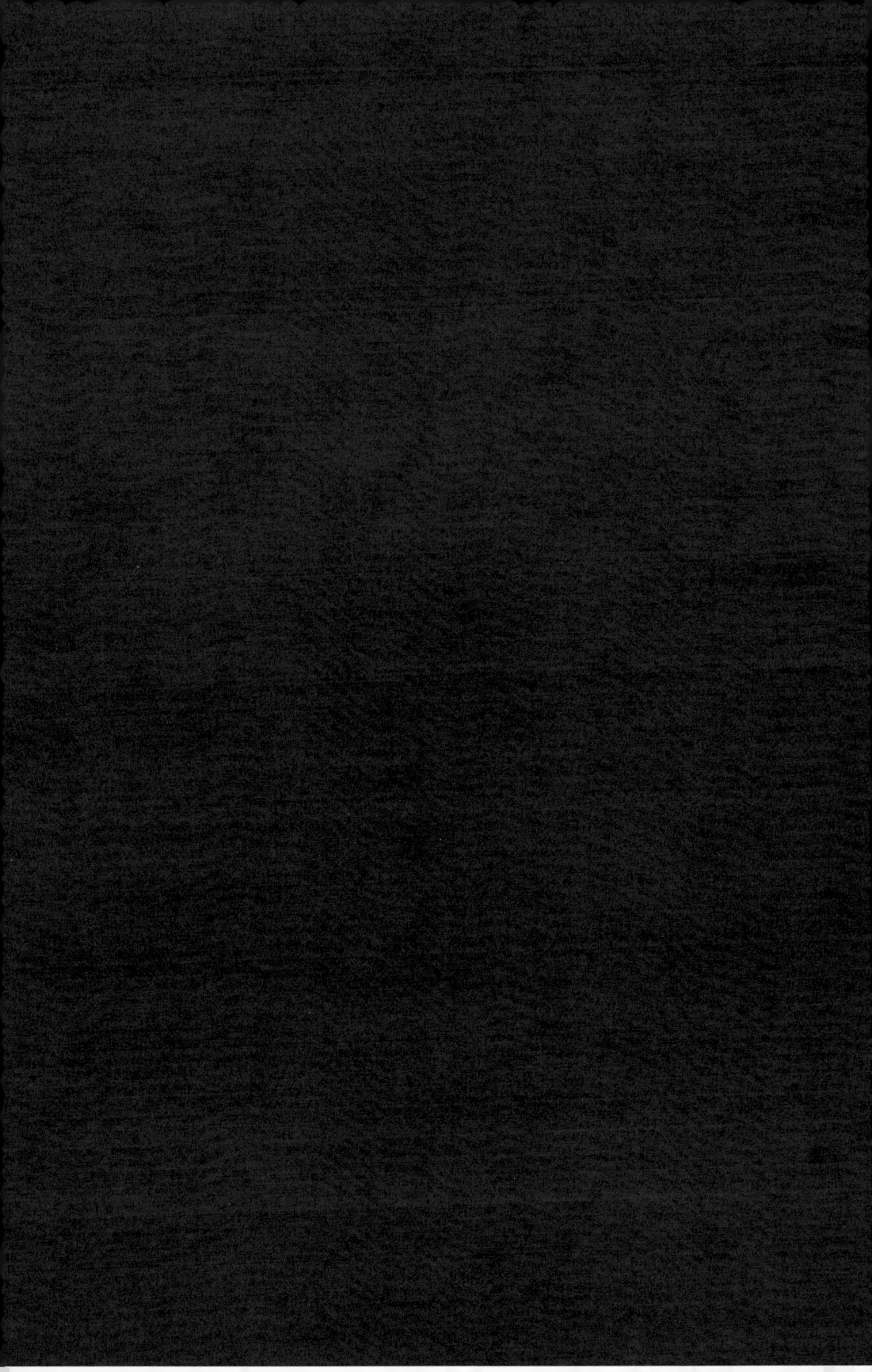

Be yourself; everyone else is already taken.
—Oscar Wilde

NEW YEAR
PUBLISHING

Feather Sharpens Iron:
The Soft Skills Need To Be Your Best
In Sales and in Life

Copyright © 2024 by New Year Publishing, LLC

144 Diablo Ranch Ct.
Danville, CA 94506 USA
http://www.newyearpublishing.com

ISBN 978-1-61431-079-2

Feather
Sharpens
Iron

The Soft Skills Needed to
Be Your Best in Sales and in Life.

Dedication

To: Hudson and Lochlan,

Nothing in this world has held a greater significance nor filled my heart more than you two beautiful boys. Your mom and I love you so very much and we hope that we're doing our best to emulate the skills within this book for you both. Never forget to stand up for those who need standing up for and that life is very hard, so make sure you're powerfully soft! 🍀

Contents

Preface

"Feather sharpens iron," conveys a contrasting concept. It suggests that even something seemingly soft, delicate, or gentle like a feather can have a positive impact on something strong and rigid like iron. It implies that sometimes subtle or unexpected influences can bring about positive change or improvement, and that strength can be found in unlikely or unexpected places. It encourages looking beyond traditional notions of strength and being open to diverse perspectives and influences that can contribute to personal growth and development.

—Author Unknown, ChatGPT

Just as I finished writing this book, ChatGPT was (and is) becoming all the talk. I was curious to see what all the fuss was about after I thought (quite confidently) that I had come up with the title "Feather Sharpens Iron" all on my own. I thought I was being creative attempting to play with that phrase and make it my intellectual property. Yep, "Feather Sharpens Iron," all mine! Turns out, it's a phrase and concept that someone, somewhere has previously defined. Or at least ChatGPT knew it. I had never read, nor heard it before in my life, so of course if I hadn't heard of it, it must be original (ouch). Oh well, it's my duty to come clean with that for those of you who haven't heard this phrase and were curious as to WTF the title means.

As I adapt the concept of feather sharpens iron as ChatGPT previously identified, my title implies that unexpected influences can bring about positive change or improvement (soft skills: likability, stronger relationships) and that strength can be found in unlikely expected places (soft skills: listening and empathy). It encourages looking beyond traditional notions of strength (technical or industry specific knowledge, rigid systems, and processes) and being open to diverse perspectives and influences (team participation, empathy, listening, and creativity) that can contribute to personal growth and development.

In an article titled, What Is the Difference Between Hard Skills and Soft Skills, Walden University's School of Lifelong Learning defines hard and soft skills: "Hard skills are job-related competencies and abilities that are necessary to complete work, while soft skills are personal qualities and traits that impact how you work. Hard skills are often applicable to a certain career; soft skills are transferable to any type of job." Just as hard skills (i.e. electrical engineering, copywriting, data mining, and CPR to list a few) can be learned, so too, can soft skills.

If you're a data person and want a little to help you get on board with the importance of soft skills, check out the information below.

● Ian Siegel, Co-founder, and CEO of ZipRecruiter stated in The Job Market Outlook for Grads: Class of 2022 that an overwhelming majority 93% of employers say "soft skills play a critical role in their decision about whom they want to hire."

● According to LinkedIn's Report, The 2023 Most In-Demand [Soft] Skills List:

⇨ Management
⇨ Communication
⇨ Customer Service
⇨ Leadership
⇨ Sales

● Based on studies from 2018-2023 by NACE, the National Association of Colleges and Employers, communication skills, problem solving, leadership and teamwork (interpersonal skills) ranked as the most important skill set employers are looking for in a new hire ■

Why use profanity in real life and in writing? Because sometimes 'darn it' just doesn't cut it.

—Jacqueline Patricks

There will be profanity within these pages. Heads up, if you don't like it, unfortunately this book may not be for you. I use profanity and have for a long time. I even use it in sales meetings and on first calls. It's a small portion of my vocabulary and just how I talk. It's my voice. I prefer speaking with people who also use profanity when appropriately applied at the right times and places. I would argue that a certain degree of profanity is essential to come across and earn trust quickly in a business environment, again the emphasis being at the right time and right place. In addition, I've read that there's been legitimate research done on people who use profanity and that they tend to be of higher intelligence and show signs of being more honest and creative. A 2006 study published in Social Influence found that obscenity and swearing had the effect of making people think the speaker was more intense and persuasive—but interestingly, it didn't affect their credibility. No shit!

There's always a risk if you use a four-letter word or something a little "lighter" in a conversation with a person you've never met, although when used at the proper place in conversation, the risk is well worth the return. When I look back over my 22 years in sales, I can recall only one time that my use of profanity created an issue. Ironically, I was on a call with a vendor who absolutely screwed up my order so bad, that my client was "line down" in production and I was being held to the fire as a result. For those of you who may be unfamiliar, "line down" is a term used when your mistakes or issues cause your customer's production line to shut down. This is also one of the worst things you can do to a customer's business. When I called the vendor, I was upset and in an extremely agitated state. This was an instance where 100% of the fault and blame was on my vendor in the sales process. When I began to explain how upset I was and how much stress I was under due to their negligence, the man on the other end of the line displayed a total lack of urgency and through his words and tone minimized the issue. I believe I stated something to the effect of "John, you need to un-fuck this right now. We gotta find a way to solve this problem quickly and creatively. I'm sorry ain't gonna work!" Much to my surprise, John replied, in a very dry and serious tone, "Please don't use profanity when you speak with me."

Have you ever seen or read the phrase, "Never in the history of calm down, has someone calmed down?" When someone is upset and uses profanity and the other person replies with "Please don't use profanity when speaking with me," or some variation of this, the SAME RESULT OCCURS! They're almost identical in their trigger response. Please note this is in general, not when directed at an individual specifically. For example, "I can't fucking believe you guys missed the ship date!" versus "You're a fucking moron and should be fired for missing the ship date!" A personal attack is the exception here and should be avoided. I feel confident that I speak for most folks when I tell you that those rare people who choose to interrupt a rant or moment of anger to let you know that using profanity isn't necessary, only end up hearing more of it, not less. Maybe that's just me and I should just calm down...

If you're a "swearer" and believe that your use of profanity is acceptable and something you're not willing to let go of, then read this next sentence carefully. Should you someday connect with another person who lets you know after your first expletive, that they would appreciate it if you don't use profanity, you can consider this person a non-starter for your business ambitions. If they're a buyer or a stakeholder in a company that you're hoping to penetrate, it's highly improbable you will do so. Why would you want to? My 22 years of sales have taught me many things, but perhaps none so clear as the importance of being able to be authentic and true to yourself in the relationship-building process. If someone is so uptight that they quickly tell you that they don't/can't tolerate profanity, do you really want to spend hours, weeks, and months, inside and outside of business trying to connect? I'm not bitter; I'm just letting some newer, younger folks in sales know that should you ever stumble upon this kind of guy or gal, keep moving. There are plenty of normal, fun swearers out there that you can call on! I promise, there ARE more fish in the sales sea and sometimes you need to cut your line quickly. It's more than ok to use "hard" words to improve your soft skills.

I guarantee those of you who read this book and sincerely and actively engage in improving your soft skills, as instructed, will increase your sales, and lead a better life. The key words are sincerely and actively. Some of you may have great soft skills while others may not feel as though yours are good enough. Do a self-evaluation to determine which soft skills are your strongest and weakest. Whichever category you fall into, this book will kick start immediate, sustained, and long-term positive gains.

This book is written based on my past and continued education as well as my personal and professional experiences in the field of sales over the past two decades plus. I've purposefully been repetitive in a few chapters and thoughts. This was done to increase familiarity and retention of these concepts. My end goal is that you'll find some moments that feel personal for you, those "aha" moments we strive to find as readers. I hope when you turn the last page of this book, your professional perspective, experiences, and sales will begin to improve quickly. Should you discover upon completion that your personal relationships also begin to improve, that too, may have been intentional ∎

Oh Craps!

Just be what you are and speak from your guts and heart - it's all that a man has.

— Hubert Humphrey

If you've ever played the table game craps before, you know that when seven comes up on the dice it's significant. Let's look at the number seven quickly. How do we get there with a pair of dice? We can roll any of the following combinations: a four and a three, a five and a two, or a six and a one. All three dice combinations are separate and distinct from one another; however, they all end up at the same number and outcome. One pairing is not better than the others, simply a different face on the same object that gives us an identical outcome. Rarely in life, in business, or in relationships is there one best way to do something, say something, write something, or in this example, roll something. There have been countless books written about sales, how to be a better salesperson, what to say, how to say it, and on and on. If we acknowledge that sales or some version therein has been around since the beginning, then naturally there will be lots of positions that have been taken by others on what works best. The intent of this book isn't to dismiss all those who've come before me, nor to imply my thoughts, tips, and suggestions are the only way to approach your sales style and skill set. Using the craps example, let's just say those before me rolled a four-three or a five-two and I'm rolling a six-one.

What follows is my roll. Throughout my sales journey, I noticed I was often perceived as an anomaly, both in comparison to my peers and in my own self-reflection. I often did things my way and had many different approaches to how I sold. There'll be many times throughout your sales adventures that your gut tells ya to do something different than your head. I recommend you learn, sooner rather than later, to trust your gut and your instincts. Don't distrust these feelings just because of a failure or two. If your gut is telling you to do something but your head is trying to stop it, take some chances for the purpose of being unique. I once heard someone say that being different is better than being better. Rather than allowing yourself to be restricted by the fear of failing, acknowledge that there are always different ways to get to an answer. It's up to you to decide which way you wanna go. Your roll, your way.

I've been in packaging sales for 22 years, primarily packaging distribution sales. I remember my very first business trip to China. The year was 2007, and I was going to visit the manufacturing plant that produced all the poly bags that Callaway golf was using worldwide. One of the many ironies in my life is that I was arguably one of the largest sales reps in the U.S. golf industry for 12+ years (based on a variety of accounts, SKUs, as well as volume). And yet, I don't own a set of golf clubs and I've never played 18 holes from start to finish. Nevertheless, over to China I flew with my

vendor rep. I felt like I was a big-time international business traveler, and I had some spring in my step. After we settled into the hotel, my vendor rep asked me if I'd like to go shopping as we had a free afternoon. I replied that I would and asked if he knew of a place where I could look at replica high-end luxury watches. He replied, "Yeah, I know a place, but China has cracked down on the sales of all counterfeit luxury items, especially watches so we're going to have to walk a bit." "Ok, let's do it," I replied. We walked several blocks through the streets of Hong Kong winding through several alleys, into a tall apartment building and up in an elevator to the 15th floor. We walked down a long hallway with a couple turns and stopped at a door. We knocked on the door, and someone looked through the eye hole and said something in Chinese. My associate gave the appropriate reply and the door opened. At this point my mind was spinning; it was a bit surreal. What the hell were we doing and what did I commit to? We then walked into a very ornate apartment with nothing out of place and no inhabitants. We continued walking back towards the bedroom door, a slot slid open on the door panel, and a pair of eyes looked at us through the opening. The door was opened with an electronic buzzer, and we stepped through. Upon entering, we stood inside a very well-lit makeshift retail space. All the glass cabinets showcased hundreds of counterfeit luxury watches. Admittedly, I'm not sure if I found the watch search experience interesting, dangerous, or humorous. I can tell you that I needed a few moments to gather my thoughts and sort out what the hell just happened. Not 60 seconds later, it was time to shop and let the negotiating begin!

17

I found a watch and settled on a price after what felt like 45 minutes of bargaining. Just before I handed over my money, I asked the gentleman I was bargaining with, "Hey what if this thing breaks right away, can I come back and get another before I return to U.S.?" He looked at me dead face, straight on and replied loudly in his broken English, with a tone of agitation as if I just stole from him, "No, if watch break, it still right two times every day!" I paused for a moment, ensuring I had just heard him correctly. Then I broke out in laughter and took his reply to mean it was time to get out.

This adventure serves simply as reminder: whatever your experience, training, or style, regardless of whether you agree, disagree or flat out don't see it, even broken watches are right, twice a day! Perhaps I'm the broken watch. Maybe others are, either way there is some right in everything and everywhere throughout a successful sales career.

It's embarrassing to scroll through social media and see how many "sales professionals" matter-of-factly tell you how you're doing it wrong, their way is the best, etc. If you take nothing away from this book, remember this:

There isn't just one best way to sell, to display soft skills, to present, or to do any single responsibility needed or required in sales.

There just isn't. Sure, there could be best practices and some methods may yield a specific type of person better results. Don't succumb to this marketing foolishness. Different salespeople (and customers) respond to and are attracted to different techniques, styles, and approaches. Even those sales guys and gals that do things their way, without any foundation in the most basic of sales practices can succeed. Broken watches are right twice a day.

I simply want to point out that social media (a major influencer for most folks) can have you second, third, and seventh guessing yourself at every stop. You'll find yourself questioning if you're doing things successfully or if you're doing anything correctly at all. Someone on social media advises going right for 30 colorful seconds, another suggests going left for 20 black and white seconds, another presents charts to validate their approach mixed with an unfamiliar study. All quick video clips and soundbites that send mixed messages and confuse you more than help you. Welcome to marketing ladies and gentlemen. Marketing from an individual who has more balls than the average person or has paid a third party to make them appear as they do. Nothing more.

As obvious as this may be to some of you, it bears repeating and highlighting. I want you to understand that your soft skills, or improving your soft skills is the best way to increase your sales. Long before you pick up the playbook of someone who is selling what worked for them, you must, MUST be familiar, comfortable and on your way to utilizing and getting better and stronger with your soft skills! They lay the foundation for success professionally and per-sonally. The better you understand and increase your soft skills, the less you'll ever need to read another sales book, buy another ticket to a retreat, or subscribe to a weekly e-mail giving you all the ways to overcome objections.

Be yourself. Authenticity trumps cool every time.
—Craig Groeschel

Be yourself and believe in yourself! If you need to practice improving your soft skills, do it. They can be learned and fine-tuned if you're willing to put in the energy and practice. Too many of us lack self-confidence and feel as though we don't have the natural ability to become something we want. Think you can't and you won't. Think you can and you're on the way there. It all starts with telling yourself you can improve your soft skills. We're our own worst enemy and we know it. I once read a quote that stated, "You believed in Santa Claus for 10 years, believe in yourself for 15 minutes."

Ok, there are certainly training courses you can pay for and subscribe to folks who are experienced and informative, I'll concede that yes, sometimes they can be helpful. They just become less necessary once you realize that being authentically you, displaying empathy, creativity, charisma and actively listening to your clients (to name a few) is what will separate you from the pack and fully open the door to sales opportunities and personal relationship growth. Soft skills aren't tricks, they're treats and skills that can be learned, and turned into character traits.

> **I've always loved the idea of not being what people expect me to be.**
>
> —Dita Von Teese

My Story,
Positively Negative

**He who laughs at himself, never runs
out of things to laugh at.**
—Epictetus

**My life's purpose is to be
a cautionary tale for others.**
—Author Unknown

To help drive home the point of mastering soft skills, I want to expose some of my own character weaknesses and by extension, the challenges I've faced over my two-decade+ sales career. Notice my vulnerability and admission of weaknesses that follow. I want to illustrate several challenges I've faced for the sake of emphasizing my point and hopefully resonating with readers that may have had similar struggles.

I'm not a reader. Never have been. I don't admit this with any sense of pride. Ironically, as far back as I can recall in elementary school, I've read at an advanced level. I was and have always been able to read very well. It's the comprehension of all the words, and the attention necessary to understand all that is intended, that I've failed at and subsequently run from. I'm not ADD, although I could be ACD (no such thing of course), which is my way of admitting I am not clinically defined ADD, but perhaps I'm close. At least I'd surrender to that label. Let me connect why my lack of interest in reading books is relevant for two important reasons.

First, to prospect in sales (seek out new customers), to advance in your industry, or to just about become better in anything, some reading is essential. When you don't enjoy reading and don't enjoy spending time reading books (when you can watch the film), it's a real pain in the ass.

Secondly, anything in this book that I've seen somewhere else or read somewhere else or gotten an idea from "else" will be admitted and pointed out. I'm neither interested in a deep dive nor intellectual formality in this book. I won't be footnoting, using a professional format, or striving for literary perfection. I'm intensely focused on writing this as if I were sitting across from you engaged in a conversation with a drink in our hands (read this from here on out as we're just sipping our third drink each.

Apologies in advance to all if I fail to remember your name if using your thoughts or words, I'll do my very best to give credit where I can. I don't have the time nor research team to assist in gathering every name, video, course, or piece of information that has opened my eyes or assisted me in understanding some areas within the themes that I'll be discussing. So, it may be general, but I'll always let ya know when anything I write isn't a Sullivan original, if in fact it's someone else's. Just wanted to give you a heads up that I'm going to be honest on every page.

I'm not a numbers guy. As far back as I can remember, I've been bad at math. I was horrible in statistics in college; luckily the second time was the charm. I can't really read an excel spreadsheet (that well). I'm not a data person. Believe me, I wish the hell I was. If I had this skill, I would've accomplished much more in my formal education as well as within my professional career. Metaphorically speaking, I've carried a piano on my back up my sales career mountain because of being challenged in this area. In a life lived to date with almost no regrets, almost none, this is a talent I've always envied.

I'm not an afternoon person. Long ago I realized I did my best work from 7:00 am to noon. Maybe it's my sleep apnea, maybe it's the 27,000 milligrams of caffeine consumed upon waking. Regardless, it's just my professional "prime time." Imagine having to schedule around my best time of the day versus the rest of the business world, who very often prefer meetings in the afternoons. Not the easiest task when you're relatively worthless from about 1:30 pm to 4:30 pm. If I fail to mention this later in the book, make sure that you understand your "prime time" each day and do all you can to schedule the most important meetings and tasks in this window. I know it seems like common sense; however, I've managed several newer guys and gals that didn't make this connection until I suggested it.

I'm not a patient person. When I hear the word "patient," the first thing I think of are the people seeing a doctor. The meaning and importance of patience was never imparted to me. I have the patience of an adolescent boy and this deficiency, too, has hurt me tremendously along my journey. This is a skill I simply haven't been able to master, and I've really tried. Sadly, my improvements have been moderate, at best. I'm revealing this only to paint the most accurate picture of a person who has been very successful relying exclusively on soft skills. In the world of sales, there are short sales cycles and long sales cycles. Throughout my career, I've been involved in the latter. Hurry the fuck up and wait, took on a whole new meaning. Watching my inbox and telephone simultaneously was a daily habit that took me almost two decades to quit.

I'm not a detail-oriented individual. I find it nearly impossible to recall a moment in my life when I took the time to patiently review details before making decisions. Since I could hold a tape, I've never been the measure twice, cut once guy. Ready. Fire! Aim. That's the way I've lived for better, and many times, for worse. Do I recommend this for you? No way!

Why then am I letting you know? Because emphasizing and illustrating my weaknesses will help demonstrate my main point, which is the critical need to have great soft skills.

Let me give you an example of my lack of detail-orientation. As I mentioned, I'm in packaging sales. If I meet you in a lobby and you ask what I sell and I reply "Packaging," what's the first thing that comes to mind? Boxes, I bet. Yep, good old brown boxes that most of us refer to as cardboard boxes. In the industry we call them corrugated boxes. I've sold several millions of dollars of cardboard, oops, corrugated boxes.

One acronym that represents the most common brown box style is RSC. This stands for Regular Slotted Container. It's the most popular box style; it's the one that has four flaps on top, two shorter, two a little longer—that's an RSC. Do you know how long it took me to recognize and understand what this acronym meant? I used it on a weekly basis and tossed it around like I was Bob Box. But I was seven years into my packaging sales career and selling thousands of regular slotted containers before I knew what RSC stood for. I still recall my first sales manager stating, "Damn it Sullivan, you really don't know what RSC stands for? You've been selling boxes for the past seven years!"

I'm not a technical expert in packaging. No one would
consider me a technical expert. By no one, I mean the number zero. I had fellow salespeople in my office and company, who were educated packaging engineers and many who weren't. But many of these people could also spec out any box on the spot and tell you everything you needed to know about it immediately. They knew what RSC meant and could say Regular Slotted Container in their sleep. Me? Not for a million dollars—not in my first seven years, anyway.

I can tell you a startling number of times when I didn't have the technical answer for a client on the spot that I should have (and could have) with some simple prep work (reading ugh) and information gathering. Although I've never been technically sound or at least where I should be in packaging materials, I've always, always succeeded in sales based entirely on my interpersonal and relationship-building skills. I'm not advocating that any of you reading this book follow my path in this regard. I've had a very successful career in packaging sales because of my interpersonal soft skills and sincere interest in others.

I've also been fortunate to have a higher-than-average ability to read people and pick up on the social queues necessary to build relationships sincerely and quickly. I've been lucky and observed many times throughout my career that people have requested me personally and wanted me to be their point of contact for a variety of reasons, all of which revolved around my soft skills, not my technical knowledge or understanding of the product. The truth is, if I ever was technically proficient in all the ways I could've and should've been (based on my sales experience and the sheer number of different packaging materials I've sold) I would have retired by now.

If you're one of the rare individuals who has both above average soft skills and hard skills, then you'll increase your chances of success tenfold. Those who fall into this category, with the right desire and ambition, would be what I consider the very best person for sales. I'd love to hire these types of folks, it's just that they're rare. In general, solid soft skills and hard skills are seldom found in one individual. If you are this person, congratulations! If you come across this type of salesperson, hire them!

If you can become this type of salesperson, do it now!

How on earth did I get into a sales career? I was waiting on an academy slot for what was then my dream job, the DEA. A freak accident subsequently left me with a partially paralyzed left foot and that opportunity quickly evaporated. One day my roommate invited me to a party in Laguna Beach, CA to the home of his regional sales manager. I attended the party with absolutely zero interest, anticipation, or pretense of working in a sales job. After all, I had always thought I was going into law enforcement and at that time being a salesperson carried nothing but negative connotations in my mind. Let alone packaging sales! Get the fuck outta here. I couldn't even bear to bring myself to tell someone I sold boxes. Ha! *Never.*

We arrive at this party in one of the coolest, swankest bachelors pads I've ever been in. This stunning home left an impression on me I'll never forget. Each of the three levels had floor to ceiling, side-to-side walls of glass looking out over Laguna Beach and the Pacific Ocean. The views from inside this mountain home were so clear and unobstructed that when looking out at the farthest area of the ocean, where the water met the skyline, you could see what appeared to be the curvature of Earth. The party began to unfold and for whatever reason, it was one of those nights where just about everything I said and did was gathering an audience and causing laughter. I could feel that I was making a positive first impression. Most extroverts have had one of these nights where you feel "on" the entire time. Completely organic and total luck that this night around total strangers, I was experiencing my most "on of ons."

Fast forward to the next morning. My roommate got a call from his sales manager who was at the party. His sales manager, who would go on to become the most influential sales mentor I've ever had, asked my roommate if I would be interested in coming in to talk about working for the company. I thought my roommate was fucking with me at first. He kept going and told me that Michael, the sales manager, was serious and thought I would make an excellent salesperson. Not only did Michael make this observation from the previous night, but the regional sales manager did as well. Keep in mind, I was still under the spell of the incredible home that the regional sales manager owned and daydreaming about what the hell it is that these guys did so they could afford that type of place and lifestyle. I told my roommate that I'd go meet with the sales manager the following day.

Prior to the meeting, I called up my father and I said, "Dad, these guys I met at a party want to possibly hire me to be a packaging salesman. I really don't have any interest but they're cool guys. What do ya think?" My dad replied, "J, if these guys see something in you, why not go meet with 'em and give it a try?" Post injury, I was planning on going back to school to get my teaching certificate and become a teacher/football coach. My dad added, "You can always go back to school and get your certificate to teach. Why not take a chance here and interview with these guys? If they see it, and they're as successful as you've seen, why not go listen to them with an open mind? Maybe this was meant to be? I think you would be a tremendous salesman." That phone call with my father was the catalyst for me to take the first step. I met with my soon-to-be sales manager and regional sales manager and was won over by their interpersonal skills, their commitment to their positions and, of course, a little, by their outward signs of financial success (thank you from the bottom of my heart Michael and Ori).

On a skepticism scale of one to ten (with one being totally skeptical and non-believing) that it was attainable for me to become a successful salesperson, I had the self-confidence and interest of a three. My managers told me that the average salesperson in the company took about three to four years to turn their work into real money. I heard it but didn't really pay attention and thought it was bullshit. Regardless, I joined the company in the fall of 2001. To say I wasn't dedicated was an understatement. I embarked on my sales journey with one oar in the water, and slightly in the water at that.

Aside from my fatalist, skeptical attitude, and the remarkably low draw check I was receiving, my father had been diagnosed with terminal cancer and given two years to live a couple weeks after I accepted the position. I immediately asked him to please move in with my fiancé and me and he willingly agreed. Thankfully, my fiancé (now wife) was supportive as I failed to ask her thoughts on the matter before I asked my father. It was a very rough and lean two years and my father passed away while witnessing my professional struggles that had a direct impact on my relationship with my fiancé.

Sadly, at just about the end of year three on the job, I hit my stride and money began coming in. There are so many things I wish my father, who passed in my arms at the age of 61, could have seen. I honestly never thought that one day in my life I could make more money on a single commission check than I had working for 12 months as a probation officer (a job wherein I interviewed some of society's worst people). What was conveyed by my managers that I initially thought was bullshit, had come true. I was staring at the largest single check made out to me that I'd ever seen. This was one of those moments I'll certainly never forget and one that will forever mean more to me because I never really believed in myself or the process. I wish my father could have cashed one of those checks with me, just once. Dad, thank you for gently suggesting I go meet with Michael and Ori. It turned out that you were exactly right.

I truly believe that mastering your soft skills is the single most important thing you can do to ensure a successful sales career. A successful and fulfilling life for that matter.

What we know matters but who we are matters more.
—Brene Brown

Let's recap: I don't like reading, numbers, or analyzing data. I'm not a technical person by any stretch of the definition. I run from details and am very impatient. I can't work for shit in the afternoons. There are plenty more weaknesses, but I'd prefer to leave some to the imagination. How in the hell does someone go into sales within the top five largest industries in the world with so many challenges and succeed? The answer is exactly what pushed me to write this book.

Soft Skills

At this point, let me assure you that I'm not implying that you should simply be likable and that's all that matters. However, I am asserting that excellent hard skills (technical skills and knowledge) and excellent soft skills (interpersonal skills) are NOT equally important to employers or moreover to your success in sales, and certainly not in life. In fact, I'm a living example of having little to no technical skill. I thrived in the most challenging of business models, which included 100% commissions, zero leads, zero lead generation, essentially zero marketing support, within an insanely saturated global industry. And yet, in spite of all of the professional challenges and personal weaknesses, I achieved tremendous success. You may think, and some who know me well certainly do, that I'm the broken watch and an outlier. I would disagree.

I just shared several of my weaknesses and I've tried to provide a glimpse of my journey in sales. My hope is to increase the chances that you'll appreciate, if not relate to the importance of soft skills. Recognizing the burdens I've had since childhood, yet finding ways to overcome them and succeed were/are due to my soft skills. Ideally, something resonates in this book that helps you make the decision and effort to improve your soft skills to better your sales career and life. Perhaps you may possess some of the same character traits or challenges that I do, so that this read may be even more interesting and personal. Imitation may be the best form of flattery, but identifying with a trait or a trial is the best way to capture attention ∎

To share your weakness is to make
yourself vulnerable; to make yourself
vulnerable is to show your strength.

—Criss Jami

Staying vulnerable is a risk we have to take
if we want to experience connection.

—Brené Brown

"Limp-athy"
Empathy

And that someone else's pain
is as meaningful as your own.
—Barbara Kingsolver

Look at this picture. Before I get into the story let me describe the photo. This is me driving a car at 4:50 am (yes, taking an irresponsible selfie) while Mohammed, my passenger, is in the backseat.

Now, I'd like to tell ya about it. I had just recently accepted a new position with a company located in San Antonio, TX. I scheduled an Uber ride to the Indianapolis airport for my second trip to the new gig. I've scheduled numerous early morning Uber rides for professional and personal travel and the early morning rides have always gone smoothly. On a side note, but relevant, I hate flying. Although I fly more than the average person, I really dislike it. In fact, I get what's frustratingly known around my house as "pre-flight anxiety" a day or two before I travel. Anyways, I scheduled my pickup at 4:30 am and every time prior, my Uber driver arrives 10-20 minutes early. Not this time.

At 4:35 am I received a text that my Uber driver couldn't get through our gate. I had texted 30 minutes earlier the exact code and instructions. So, I called the driver as soon as I read the text. He picked up the phone and I could immediately tell English was not his first language. I was already a little frustrated, as one, he was slightly late, and two, I was in my heightened pre-flight anxious state. I tried to walk him through it, and he didn't understand anything I was saying. I hung up the phone and texted him the instructions again.

Ten minutes later, as I'm standing on my porch with the porch light on, I see his car driving very slowly towards my home. He was driving at a snail's pace when he slowly passed me (even though I was standing with suitcases in front of the only house with a light on in the neighborhood). He puts the car in reverse and drives into my driveway. 15 minutes late. He exits his vehicle and hands me his phone while I'm putting my suitcase in his trunk. He says something to the effect of, "I don't know where go. Please write." I'm a bit startled that my driver doesn't know that he's taking me to the airport, or how to use his phone for his directions and route. After all, he's an Uber driver.

Here's where it really takes off. As I'm not very tech savvy (to put it very kindly) and I've never used the Uber app from the driver's viewpoint, I quickly handed his phone back and told him that I'll give him verbal directions. He smiles and we get in the car. Off we go at 4:50 am, 20 minutes late and my anxieties are increasing. We get to the first stop sign, and I tell him to please turn left. He turns right. I tell him he made the wrong turn, to no avail as he simply didn't understand. In case that sailed over your head, we're talking about understanding a right turn from a left turn with my UBER DRIVER! So, we arrive at the next stop sign, and I tell my driver to turn left. He turns right. Now, my blood pressure is boiling. We finally exit my neighborhood and we're on the side road heading out towards the freeway. In my city there are numerous roundabouts. It's 4:55 am and still dark and as we approach a roundabout, he reduces his speed to one mph or so. Fortunately, there were no other vehicles on the road to contend with. We crawl around the round-about and just as we straighten out on the road, I aggressively tell him to pull over. "Pull the fuck over right here!" The driver pulls over and I loudly tell him to get out, hand me his keys, and sit in the passenger seat. He hands me his keys and says what I believe to be something like, "Good, please you drive."

I get in the driver's seat, and he opens the door and jumps in the back seat of the car, even though I'm slamming my hand down on the passenger seat signaling him to sit next to me. Nope, in the back he goes, seatbelt on. Off I go. And go I went. The time is now 5 am and I'm running late enough to miss my flight. My blood pressure is soaring, my anxieties are at a fever pitch, and I hit the gas. I take his little car to 90 mph on the freeway and it's still dark and relatively traffic free. As I'm speeding along, I'm yelling at him in the back in a series of statements that go like these: "How in the fuck did you get your driver's license?" "How in the hell did you pass the damn security screening and test to get your Uber permit?" "Do you have any idea what I'm saying to you?" "What in the fuck, FUCK!"

A mile or so down the freeway after taking a very deep breath, I asked my driver his name and he understood this question. He replied his name was Mohammed. I asked him where he's from and he also knew this question. He replied he was from Pakistan. These would be the only two questions he could answer in English. While speeding along at 90 mph, I start trying to teach Mohammed an English lesson. I hold my right hand up and repeat, right. After my fourth time holding and saying it and pointing in the rear-view mirror for him to repeat it, he says it. Same lesson with my left hand, only needed three times for him to repeat and play along. At this moment, I'm seeing red and am furious. I'm yelling at him the entire time because it's loud in the small car as the engine is pushed to a high RPM level. I'm very anxious to be flying, I'm very angry that I may miss the flight that I'm fucking anxious to take, and I can't believe how little English he speaks. I should note, I've always been very patient and empathetic to foreign speakers in our country. However, at this point I may be missing my flight for my second rotation on my new job, I'm tired, and it's early – did I mention, I was anxious too?

Take another look at the close-up of Mohammed in the backseat. The resolution doesn't do his look much justice, but I think you'll see that he's afraid. As we raced into the airport, I slammed the car in park, and I look back at Mohammed and I see his face. I made up some time driving to the airport at a high speed and have a good chance of making my flight. I jump out of the car, grab my suitcase and Mohammed is standing there repeating with his head titled down, "I'm sorry. I'm sorry. I'm sorry." I can see that he is still afraid. It was at this moment that my empathy kicked in.

I recognized that he didn't speak English, so it was impossible for him to articulate anything to me. I could also clearly see I had frightened him with my driving and yelling. I walked up to him and while I extended my hand to shake his, I simultaneously put my other hand on his shoulder. I paused while looking at him directly in his eye and said, "Mo, I'm sorry for yelling and speeding. I know you won't understand my words exactly, but I know you can tell I'm trying to apologize in my language. Thank you for allowing me to be your Uber driver. I can now add this to my resume." I smiled, Mo smiled and said, "Thank you." I anxiously walked into the airport and made my flight.

Sincere empathy requires that we maintain the ability to put ourselves in others' shoes no matter what the situation or crises. We can't simply express or display empathy during times of calm when very little is on the line. It's the moments in life that rattle us, that jangle our nerves, or cause us to blow an emotional fuse that test our true ability to be empathetic.

I'll never forget my morning with Mo, the Uber driver, for two very distinct reasons. The first is obvious in that I commandeered someone's damn vehicle to make my flight. I didn't think twice about it and in retrospect I could have easily been attacked or hurt us both due to my emotional state and hyper driving. The second is why I wanted to share this adventurous and unique story. I'm proud that under stress and with all the things going on in my mind, I somehow found the ability to recognize that Mo hadn't done anything malicious to me and didn't intend to upset me. He was trying to earn a living, in a foreign country, by driving a car most often occupied by those that spoke a language different than his. Yes, of course he should have known what he was up against and the challenges that he would create for others. However, that has nothing to do with empathy in this example. At that very moment in time, I was able to recognize he was afraid and apologize for blowing up. Rather than tell him to fuck off as I slammed the car door, I wanted to leave this moment in time better than it came to me.

Countless books, lectures and articles have addressed and stressed the importance of empathy. Sadly, there's an unfortunate societal deficiency of it in America today. The word empathy is used so often that we've become tone deaf to its importance. I bet most salespeople know what the concept means, but I'm not sure they really, truly get it. Allow me to beat the dead horse just a little more regarding how critical it is to be sincerely empathetic in thought and action.

Empathy is the ability to emotionally understand what other people feel, see things from their point of view, and imagine yourself in their place. Essentially, it is putting yourself in someone else's position and feeling what they are feeling.

—Bailey Mariner, Very Well Mind

As I've gotten older, I've become more cynical and suspicious of others' motivations and behaviors. Consequently, my empathy, and even more significantly, that of my friends and co-workers, has begun to dull due to the daily grind of life and the totality of miles we've put on our biological odometer. For as many times as you'll hear and (one day say) how much it sucks growing old, one of the worst emotional and intellectual losses is this very decline in empathy as we age. As evidenced by the cranky old guy or gal who appears pissed off all the time; or the folks we encounter that have seemingly been irritable their entire lives. Yes, life grinds our empathy down to the nub and gradually eliminates all the fucks we have left to give. Luckily for Mo, I still have some empathetic tendencies in "my" Uber vehicle.

On the job it's become almost reflexive that when a co-worker needs time off for emotional distress or anything relating to their mental health, we roll our eyes (or at least we internally do) and instantly believe the person is "milking it," taking advantage, being less than truthful, or worse still, unable to have the strength to get over and through "it." It's quite easy to get caught up in feeling agitated or angry and transfer our own feelings of disappointment and dissatisfaction towards others as opposed to empathizing. I get it, misery does love company, or better stated, it loves a party of people.

Empathy covers so many interpersonal relationship-building bases that it's impossible to not have a sincere and significant amount of this skill if you're going to be successful in sales or life for that matter. One of the most critical areas where being significantly empathetic gives a person a major advantage is within conflict resolution. Conflict can be between you and your employer, you, and a client, or you and anyone else in your life. Imagine being able to halt and put yourself in the exact same emotional state and position the other person is in. Not just hear their problem, concern, or bitch, but transform yourself into their mind and begin to deconstruct their issue from their point of view. Is this even possible? You bet the fuck it is!

I've seen it done to me, to others and I've had the opportunity on several occasions to be the only one in a room that had the ability to display sincere empathy towards an individual's situation. Does this make me rare or unique? Of course not. However, I promise you this, I've saved a few people's jobs by having the ability to empathize and communicate states of mind, emotional states and motivations resulting therein. One of the easiest ways to reprimand or fire someone is to let our egos run wild and unchecked solely because they've been bruised. It takes self-control, self-reflection, maturity, and a shit ton of patience to pause, hold, and think about the other person's feelings, and then continue to maintain composure to find a resolution.

Additionally, empathy allows salespeople to pick up on challenges, stresses, or emotions that their clients are displaying and sincerely understand them and adjust their own behavior accordingly. By adjusting your behavior, you're recognizing an emotional state that is affecting the person with whom you are engaged. Whether this individual is consciously aware you are purposefully adjusting your behavior to display empathy or not isn't the point. Either way the result is beneficial and strongly increases your relationship. When your client perceives your consideration of their emotional state or situation, they'll recognize your emotional intelligence. Further, this subtle effort will subconsciously convey your genuine warmth and sincerity towards them. The result has a powerful impact on the person. Displaying empathy is one of the quickest ways to establish trust and by extension, a real relationship with your client. Displaying empathy is extraordinary and if you possess emotional intelligence, you've undoubtedly witnessed connecting with someone quickly because your awareness of and empathy towards their emotional state. Displaying empathy will get you on a fast track to building a strong relationship with just about anyone out there.

A mentor once told me about a physical way to display empathy during a conversation. Here's the move, if you hold your head straight up when talking with someone, you're displaying a firm, attentive, and sterile demeanor. Yes, this is standard, professional, and "serious" body language. To appear empathetic, just tilt your head slightly, especially when the person you are speaking with shares something personally or professionally important. Don't tilt your head from the moment you sit down and start speaking with someone, you'll look like your neck is kinked. Utilize the tilt throughout the meeting during the back-and-forth conversation at key moments. You'll know those moments if you're actively listening. This is a simple, but very powerful form of non-verbal communication that silently speaks to your client. What I find interesting about this head tilt is that it simply happens naturally to those who are deeply empathetic by nature. Remember, empathy can't be faked, it must be genuine and sincere. Trying to fake empathy will end in broken trust and a failed relationship.

Be authentic (always).

Find a way to understand empathy and improve yours if it's not a natural strength. It can be learned and developed through mental and emotional energy. There will be walls. Oh, there will be many voices inside your head telling you, "Fuck them. Fuck that! Why should I trust…" This is your ego blocking your drive to be empathetic. Sure, ok. I've always believed that taking the "Fuck so and so…." route is the easy path. The true challenge is taking a chance and giving a person the benefit of the doubt.

The burden is pausing to imagine what the other person is feeling but maybe not saying. Saying, but maybe not showing. Showing, but not revealing.

Being empathetic may get you burned by extending your effort and consideration to someone who is lying or pretending. Recognize, to be truly empathetic, you're accepting the risk of dealing with individuals who consistently default to lies and manipulation. We're not empathetic to keep score on our wins or losses based on our gut hunches and beliefs about other's motives. We strive to be empathetic, to display a larger sense of self and get into another's shoes at their most important personal and professional moments. We connect as humans through our ability to demonstrate empathy.

If you want to monetize the ability to have sincere empathy, you simply need to trust in its power and give it a try. Again, it takes sincerity, serious energy, and consistency. Most people who don't have it by the time you've picked up this book are going to struggle to make it a part of their mindset. It's not impossible, but it is challenging and worth every single minute you spend practicing, pausing, thinking, and empathizing before reacting. It's worth pointing out yet again, if you fake it or try to, you risk a serious backfire.

Empathy is a muscle, so it needs to be exercised.
—Satya Nadella

Empathy improves your sales success and personal success. It builds a positive mental foundation for everything we do. Salespeople who have high emotional intelligence and are skilled in empathetic approaches to relationship building will absolutely increase their sales and personal happiness. The stoic personality types that pride themselves in maintaining a strict business attitude are missing out on a great opportunity to expand their network and business. The "arms distance" approach to interpersonal professional relationships may work for some, however, they'll rarely be the most successful salespeople (or voted most wanted to take a road trip with). Empathy increases your charisma, likability, and everything about you. If you're not confident that your ability to show empathy is significant, work on it!

Think of empathy as the trunk of your soft skills tree. All branches grow and flourish from this base. It's not just a nice to have skill, it's a must-have skill.

Practical Application

• **Problem Solving:** When there's an issue, and a client is upset, you can use empathy to see the situation from the client's perspective. When you encounter issues with clients, empathy is how you can truly understand their perspective. Feeling what the client is experiencing is an excellent driver to help you address their stressful challenges quickly. Additionally, being empathetic puts you in a mental and strategic place to prepare contingency plans or begin corrective actions in advance.

• **Communication:** Salespeople who are empathetic are better communicators. They understand they may need to present ideas differently based on their client's present state. Word choice, order, and tone are extremely powerful ways to demonstrate your understanding of your client's feelings and needs.

• **Listening:** Reps who are empathetic have better listening skills. When sincerely engaging and putting yourself into the state of your client, you're more apt to be an active listener. This connection and by extension, understanding of your client, allows a salesperson to put together a custom presentation that is more likely to resonate with their target. The more you can frame your sales presentation to your client's style and needs, the more significant, powerful, and persuasive it'll be.

• **Relationship Building:** Even if your clients can't express why, displaying empathy can leave a lasting impression on them. This is because our emotional intelligence enables us to resonate with others and leave them feeling understood and valued. By demonstrating empathy towards your clients, you not only establish a positive relationship, but also have the potential to make a big first impression. Mastering the skill of empathy will help you build strong, long-lasting relationships with your clients, which leads to increased sales and long-term success.

42

• **Acknowledge and validate others' feelings.** Connect with others by making statements like, "I understand why you feel this way." Simply show others that you recognize their emotional state based on what they are sharing and expressing.

• **Notice their body language and yours.** Observe your client's gestures, eye contact, and body language and adjust yours to match/mirror theirs. The appropriate amount and length of eye contact, body language, and expressions will demonstrate to others that you're displaying empathy and in sync with them emotionally ■

Feeling too much is a hell of a lot better than feeling nothing.
—Nora Roberts

Before you criticize a man, walk a mile in his shoes. That way, when you do criticize him, you'll be a mile away and have his shoes.
—Steve Martin

I'm No van Gogh:
Creativity

> In order to be irreplaceable,
> one must always be different.
> —Coco Chanel

Business is more competitive now than it's ever been. Truthfully, it'll only become increasingly more competitive. It's always been important to be creative, however never more so than right now. I'm not referring to your artistic ability. I'm a stick figure artist and have been since I was given my first crayon. I'm talking about creativity in the sense of how you stand apart and differentiate yourself from others in everything you do in terms of behavior and interpersonal interactions. My emphasis on creativity here is intended to relate more to uniqueness, being different, standing out, separating yourself in the smallest, if not largest of ways. Being innovative in almost everything you write, text, and at times, say. Because it's more competitive out there, the sooner you recognize that expressing yourself differently than your competitors is of the utmost importance, the better!

It's better to be absolutely ridiculous than absolutely boring.
—Marilyn Monroe

In the quote above, Marilyn opted for "boring," but I'd like to tweak it slightly and replace it with "average." There's nothing wrong with average when it comes to how you rank in almost anything you like or want to accomplish. I mean after all, most of us are in fact average in the statistical sense. Yet when it comes to wanting to distinguish yourself from the other average sales reps or distinguish yourself from the average husbands, wives, friends, etc., I want you to consciously start thinking about doing, saying, and writing things differently/creatively. Take a chance, try some new things and approaches such as using new words, phrases, signature lines, greetings, handshakes, and subject lines. The list goes on and on. Ok, so you don't get the reaction or response you're hoping for, just try something different next time.

I understand some of you may be wondering about the idea of standing out and being memorable. I'm not suggesting you dye your hair purple or get a mohawk for a JP Morgan Chase presentation. Instead, consider consistently exploring new and unique ways of engaging people in person, through text, e-mail, phone calls, or any other communication method. The aim is to leave a positive and lasting impression. Demonstrating your willingness to step outside the ordinary will set you apart. Creatively separating yourself from the competition will yield rapid and remarkable results.

Of course, it's challenging and perhaps unrealistic to try and do a 180-degree change in creative direction in everything you write, do, and speak. I'm being hyperbolic when suggesting you need to be creative across the board. Specifically, you need to find a way to stand out in the very crowded party of salespeople. That's as plain as it can be stated. Average sales folks tend to stick with what they're comfortable with and rarely, if ever, stray off their script. Instead, challenge yourself to be more imaginative and adventurous in your presentations and meetings. The only time being average isn't enough is when you're in the competitive world of sales. Being ordinary is going to give you exactly what you're giving: ordinary sales accomplishments.

Ok, some salespeople are just naturally, or have been raised by example to be more unique, charismatic, and plain old interesting. Not everyone can be the life of the party and spark interest simply by trying different things. However, it starts with taking some chances. For those of you who may lack the confidence to even try new approaches, there's good news. You can learn ways to become more creative just like any other skill. It'll take those of you who automatically buy a bottle of alcohol for every single secret Santa holiday party a bit longer, but if you're open-minded and willing, you too, can learn some unique ways to distinguish yourself. Bottom line: it's time to try, at least try, to stand out. If this is uncomfortable to even think about, remember, it's not necessarily unnatural, it's most likely unfamiliar. Once you try some things out, you'll use what feels best and pick up traction from there.

One day early in my career while sitting in my office, my manager told me that there was a young lady from Cutco in the lobby. He suggested I meet with her and see what she had to offer. If you're not familiar with Cutco, it's a company that sells cutlery. I listened to the Cutco sales rep's presentation and thought, what the hell do I need with a new knife or set of knives for that matter? At this time in my life I couldn't cook, and I'm not that much better now. A longstanding joke in my family is when asked what I make best, the response is simply, "reservations."

So, as I'm listening to the Cutco rep, I'm running my client list through my head, both current and prospects that I was targeting. Who would appreciate a nice knife? Then it hit me, Wanda! I'm going to get a knife for Wanda for the holidays and I want it to be unique and different. I had absolutely no idea if Wanda enjoyed cooking or even cooked for that matter. I had a spark of inspiration, and I was going to run with it. My thought at this moment was that if I could do something creative around a carving knife, there was a good chance it would be used and looked at for many years (and holidays) to come. I asked the Cutco rep if I could have the carving knife engraved. She replied, it could be. So, I took out my credit card and ordered Wanda a brand-new carving knife just in time for the holidays. On the knife was inscribed the following:

**Merry Christmas Wanda. Thanks for all your support.
Enjoy this gift & please don't ever
put it in my back. ☺
- Jason 2006**

On a personal note, Wanda and I remain friends to this day, over 15 years since we first met and did business together. When I began writing this book, she was one of the first people I reached out to get this photo.

At the time I ordered this knife, Wanda was the person I needed to trust me, like me, and support me for current and future projects. You could say that she was the single most important person in my professional sphere at this time. I had nothing to lose as I to tried to make her laugh while simultaneously sending her a message that would last as long as that knife would…please don't give my business to someone else without giving me a chance to keep it. We worked on several projects together and while I can't say that the knife was the primary reason, I can assure you that it landed its intended "ha" factor and went a long way in developing our friendship. Maybe I'm not the only one who's ever done this, the point is that I had never heard or seen someone doing something like it before. To me, that's the creative goal. Identify something you can do, that you hadn't done or thought of before, nor seen done by other people on a regular basis, if ever. Obviously, the gift of a carving knife is not unique in terms of the object itself, however the inscription on the knife was the memorable move.

Here's another example of being unique for creative effect. One of my closest friends, Mr. Jason DeFrancesco (perhaps you've heard of him) had to give a presentation to an extremely large, well-known fruit producing company. Not only were hundreds of thousands (or potentially millions of dollars) in packaging revenue on the table, but he was also set to present to a large audience. While he was preparing for his presentation, he realized that one of the biggest hurdles in being awarded the contract was the fact that he had never produced the packaging needed for the agricultural industry. So, after we spoke and tossed out some presentation strategies, he decided to set up his slide deck for the presentation in a unique way. After his first few intro slides, he inserted a blank slide. When he advanced his presentation to the blank slide, he paused and said this to the large group of berry packaging buyers, engineers, and marketers: "This slide represents exactly how many clients I've worked with in berry companies over the past 20 years." He would, as we loosely rehearsed, let that sit and quickly glance around the room. That would be followed up with him adding, "However, I have in fact creatively developed and produced packaging in many other industries. So please allow me to illustrate all the reasons I find this to be of benefit to you all." Click-advance slide. The very next slide was a bulleted list of the top reasons not having experience in their specific industry would be helpful, creative, and not a problem.

This might not read like something that is remarkably creative, however, I promise that if you're advancing a deck presentation and purposefully put up a blank slide and combine that with speaking directly to the why it's blank, it stimulates the listeners' minds and makes your presentation creatively and uniquely more memorable. You see, the average salesperson, moreover the average person, just does the average. The average no surprises, non-creative, same as others presentation, paper, e-mail, LinkedIn message, text, voice message, proposal, thank you gift, secret Santa gift, and the list goes on....

I recently saw something that I thought was interesting. The story went something like this: when pouring a glass of water during a job interview, let it fill all the way up and run over a bit to ensure your interviewer sees it. If they say anything about you being nervous, simply reply that you always give more than required. I gotta believe that in this scenario, any candidate who had the composure and gumption to pull that one off, gets a lifetime spot in the interviewer's memory. The point of course, the overpour and quick wit when questioned about nerves is something that would be very difficult to forget.

Finally, let's look at one other creative way to stimulate someone's attention and/or interest them in learning more about you or your presentation. Suppose you're reading a book that you find interesting, helpful, and perhaps even humorous. A real page turner! You get to a certain chapter and turn the page and suddenly, it's blank. You turn to the next page and it's blank. You think to yourself something must be wrong with the final layout that wasn't caught during editing and proofreading. You turn to the third page and now you're getting a bit bent. The next page you turn has a big statement on it with the words, GOT YA on it. Or something similar. The book picks up on the next chapter after having put you through a few blank pages of WTF happened? Ya see what I'm driving at here? Put some prep time into the things you're doing that establish yourself as different than average. Show others that you're unique in a sea of sameness. Let me point that out once again, it doesn't matter if your attempt to be creative is a homerun. Your effort will be recognized, giving you mental and creative "extra credit" and may spark curiosity about your ingenuity in the sales process. You'll quickly stand out amongst your competitors. Be memorable. "You've been memorable since the day we first met..." or "I remember that time when you...I've never forgotten that." Those phrases have a nice ring to them. These examples are to give you some ideas of things I've done or seen that I feel are unique, creative and will make you more memorable. You may or may not agree with their levels of creativity. Remember, nothing you do will have a 100% creative "wow" factor or success rate. People have varying opinions and likes and dislikes. It gets even more unpredictable when you're striving for something extraordinary and attempting to separate yourself, through action, e-mail, call, or voicemail to list a few. Your intent will not always be received in the manner with which you are hoping. Well, no shit! Just wanted to state the obvious for you more sensitive types, for you are I, and I am you.

As a salesperson, expressing unique ideas can greatly benefit the team, as creative thinking stems from diverse perspectives. Creative individuals are often unafraid to venture into uncharted territories and take risks, even if it means facing potential embarrassment or loss. Their contributions can spark inspiration in their teammates, encouraging them to think outside the box and consider alternative perspectives. Innovative salespeople often possess a willingness to adapt to new ideas and processes, making them invaluable assets to any team. By challenging the status quo and pushing for experimentation, ingenious salespeople often help teams avoid falling into the trap of relying on outdated practices just because "that's the way it's always been done." Let me re-state that for emphasis. The worst sentence in the English language is in fact, "because it's/we've always done it that way." If you hear this and aren't ready to show them something that will erase that ignorant default of a philosophy, then run away from the prospect. That phrase should get a rise out of your competitive sales spirit and ensure you go the extra mile. If it doesn't, run the hell away from the prospect?

My aim for stressing creativity as a critical soft skill is to highlight ways to creatively set yourself apart from the average salesperson out there. As many of us already know, getting decision makers time and attention is becoming increasingly more challenging. Therefore, emphasizing and cultivating one's creativity can be a game-changer, enabling salespeople (people) to showcase their unique strengths and qualities that make them invaluable assets to any organization. There are many ways to improve your creativity as a salesperson, but none more important than the simple act of trying new things. Don't get in the habit of doing the same things in the same ways with your sales technique. Be unpredictably fresh and stimulate those you come in contact with by showing them you're always thinking about ways to do things better, more efficiently, and more productively. Your ideas may fall flat, or they may not work at all, but they'll most certainly separate you from your competition. If nothing else, you want your client or prospect to identify you as someone who isn't delivering their fish from the "Sea of Sameness."

I want to stress creativity in the sense of how you differentiate yourself and stand out. As previously stated, the market is remarkably competitive in business today. Reaching decision makers and connecting with shot callers can be overwhelming at times. Let me close this chapter with the perfect quote that summarizes the point.

If you always do what you always did, you will always get what you always got.
—Albert Einstein

Practical Application

• **Create a simple one-page sheet for your customers.** Collaborate with your marketing or product development teams to come up with solutions to common challenges you face in the market. For example, if you routinely hear from prospects that you have too many alternatives and options for them that they're overwhelmed, perhaps you may consider developing a simple one sheet that bullet points and simply highlights all your product(s) features and/or advantages in the marketplace.

• **Tell stories to illustrate how your product can solve problems and meet your clients' needs.** Tie relative stories to your product or service presentation. Relative stories that are told well are one of the easiest ways for us to remember anything. Bonus: Become a talented storyteller as this skill universally improves your communication.

• **Personalize your presentation and approach to introductions.** Research and prepare during discovery anything you can about your audience and company. Example, you have an upcoming meeting with a Director of Engineering, and you discover she attended the University of Michigan, maybe consider wearing a Michigan sweatshirt into the meeting. "I see you're wearing a Michigan sweatshirt; did you go to school there?" Me, "No, but I saw you did, and you better believe I ran out and bought it to try to make ya smile. I sure hope you had nothing but great memories there, otherwise I'm out the $50 bucks and have done nothing but given you a reminder for the next 30 minutes of your four years of hell."

Speaking of the Great Lakes State, once upon a time I had an important interview with a decision maker who attended Michigan State University. I presented him with a wrapped University of Michigan (serious rival) football helmet as a gift prior to our interview. To my surprise, he showed very little reaction. I was disappointed for an instant and felt almost stupid. However, I quickly realized this wasn't about me, it was simply his personality. Do I regret the effort? Absolutely not. The helmet didn't impact the interview nor outcome. I believe in taking risks and trying to separate yourself. In the end, I got the job. Sometimes you win, sometimes you lose, but the key is to play!

• **Use visual aids.** Pictures can tell 1,000 words. Great pictures can tell 10,000 words! Images have the ability to convey emotions and thoughts that sometimes words simply can't. When used effectively, great photos can tell a captivating story that resonates with your audience on a deeper level. I once witnessed a student give a presentation on the challenges of being a first-time parent by painting a vivid picture of a relatable scenario – a busy morning before work where everything goes sideways, including being vomited on by his seven-month-old baby. In that moment, he clicked on a photo in his presentation that captured the chaotic yet hilarious situation, showcasing his stained sport coat and shocked expression. It perfectly encapsulated the rollercoaster of emotions that new parents experience, and the audience couldn't help but relate and laugh along with him. Such is life. A great big beautiful hot mess of love, stress, challenge, beauty, anxiety, and pride crashing together instantaneously within a single image. These types of moments are beautiful and when you're able to display vulnerability and authenticity, you will connect with your audience (client/target) and build rapport. Be you, take chances and use whatever you can get your hands on to add flavor so that you'll be thought of as you, not as just "a salesperson."

• **Consider alternate perspectives.** Ask your teammates, managers, friends, and family (excellent choices as they often are disconnected from the norms and players thereby increasing chances for creativity) to get fresh and alternative perspectives on ideas or approaches to stimulate your clients' or targets' mind ■

Turn Handshakes Into Hugs
Charisma

> Charisma is a sparkle in people that money can't buy. It's an invisible energy with visible effects.
> —Marianne Williamson

I've read approximately five sales books in my life, maybe. Even with my dislike for reading, I was trying some things early in my career to get a spark. There's one book above the other handful that has stuck with me since I read it. This book left a major impression on me and is the primary reason I wanted to write about soft skills and their important role in succeeding in sales. The book is titled The Little Red Book of Selling by Jeffrey Gitomer. Its style and format were perfect and very appealing to the average salesperson with an attention span of just a few seconds. It was short, it was highlighted, it had all sorts of emphasized points in the margin. It had all the bells and whistles for short-attention-span-shiny-object-loving-non-readers while getting straight to the good stuff. I appreciated the book so much that I lent it to someone and of course you know what happens when we loan a book…it's gone!

All things being equal, people want to do business with their friends. And all things being NOT SO EQUAL, people STILL want to do business with their friends.

—Jeffrey Gitomer

I love quotes (as you've probably noticed). I absolutely love 'em! I'm going to use as many as I can within these pages. To me, Gitomer's quote is the "quote of all sales quotes" and speaks to my underlying sales philosophy and purpose of this book. Below is my flowchart showing charisma and its relativity to sales opportunities.

MONETIZE CHARISMA

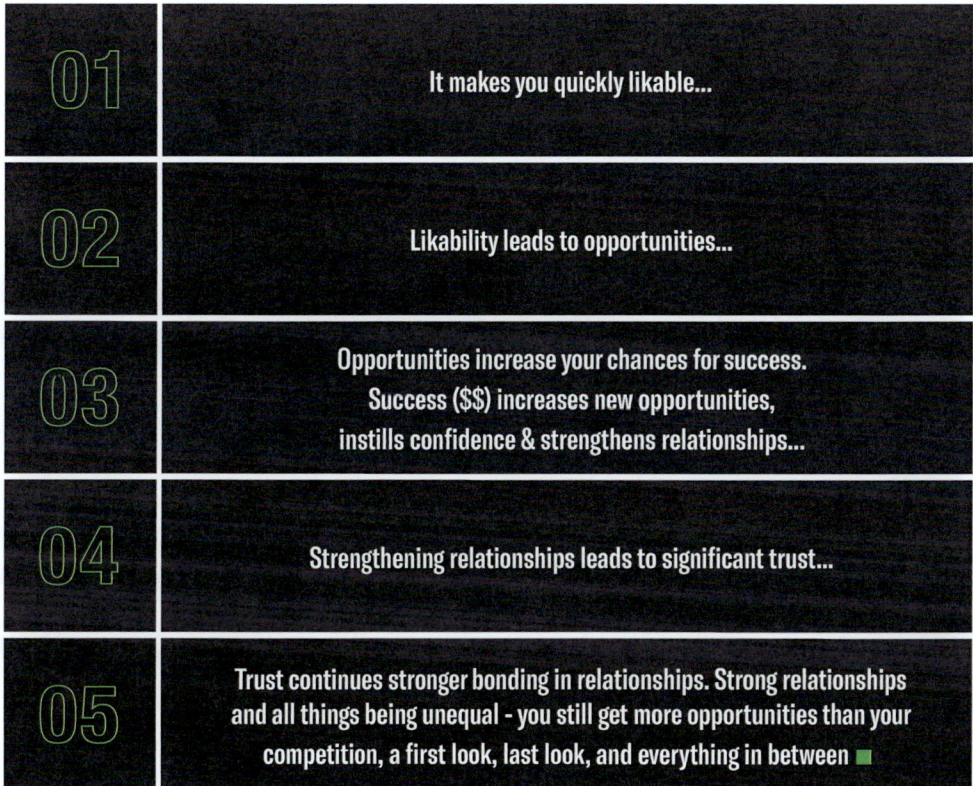

01	It makes you quickly likable...
02	Likability leads to opportunities...
03	Opportunities increase your chances for success. Success ($$) increases new opportunities, instills confidence & strengthens relationships...
04	Strengthening relationships leads to significant trust...
05	Trust continues stronger bonding in relationships. Strong relationships and all things being unequal - you still get more opportunities than your competition, a first look, last look, and everything in between ■

Having, practicing, or mastering soft skills will make you more personable, likable, and attractive in every manner. Once you recognize this, you'll have more time to build trust and develop sincere relationships and friendships with your clients. Once you become a true and trusted friend to your clients, the doors will open and open quickly. They'll stay open longer than any other door you walk through for business. This quote perfectly summarizes the reality of relationships and their importance in/on/for business.

Make no mistake about it, sincere likability and trust lead to relationships and friendships. These "...ships" ultimately develop from your soft skills. People buy from people they like and buy even more from those that rise to the definition of a friend. It's that simple. All things being unequal, people still prefer to buy from their friends, PEOPLE THEY LIKE. Because of this reality, technical skills, hard skills, and being an expert in something, are generally a secondary set of preferred or ideal skills, when it comes to either sales or relationship building. Of course, there are times when buyers can't buy from those they prefer, but it's only after exhausting every possible avenue. With a few exceptions, a technical, hard skills expert can be replaced by another technical expert. The person who has a black belt in soft skills will ultimately develop a significant relationship, or a legitimate friendship with their clients and always be a more successful and better salesperson (person). I can't make this anymore clear. I've experienced, observed, and witnessed this fact with other salespeople over the past 20+ years so many times that I'm cemented in my belief. To be fair, I don't mean to denigrate those super technical, hard skill individuals who let's say, aren't as charismatic, outgoing, and sociable as others. I just need to drive home the point that these individuals, in general, will not succeed in sales as well as those who are proficient and display great soft skills across the board.

Recently, I came across an article written by a Ph.D. in psychology claiming that charismatic people are narcissistic. I tried to look for the non-disclaimer that the author surely couldn't mean all charismatic people are narcissistic. I couldn't find it and I couldn't possibly agree with this view. Blanketing charisma with such a negative connotation without demonstrating some variance seemed both foolish and professionally irresponsible.

Speaking for myself, I'm sure someone in my life has accused me of being narcissistic at some point and time. The term is thrown around loosely and most people don't understand the correct definition. Just to make sure I wasn't completely disconnected, I did a little research on narcissism and sure enough, I'm not close to the definition. I didn't stop there though; I reached out to my former psychiatrist to double check for a potential blind spot. He assured me that although I was "other" things– I was in fact, nowhere near the definition of narcissism. The reason that I wanted to address this inaccurate connection and association between narcissism and charisma is simple. Throughout this book, I lay the foundation that being charismatic is a benefit that has very few competitors where soft skills are concerned. In addition, just like this psychologist's article, there are people who see genuinely charismatic people as being something less than real.

As far back as I can remember, I've had an easy time meeting and talking to just about anyone. When I'm engaged in a conversation or impassioned on a topic (look out) the words come naturally and flow easily. Because of this, I've often been called "full of shit." Maybe this has happened to you before and possibly more than once. For whatever reason, if someone speaks articulately, creatively, energetically, and passionately (not necessarily in that order) there can be a connection to someone being disingenuous, phony, or used-car-salesman-y. If this has happened to you, you'll know exactly what I'm discussing here in this example. If it's never happened to you, imagine believing in what you're saying so confidently and expressing it with energy and passion, to only have your listener (whoever) look at you dead face when you've finished and say, "Get the fuck outta here. You're full of shit." When speech comes easy, the interpretation is that someone has spoken or rehearsed their line(s) numerous times before and they're just inserting them into the conversation to somehow appear more _____ (insert any variety of adjectives here: intelligent, confident, humorous, prepared, and so forth).

Regardless of whether you've personally experienced this mislabeling or not, while not trying to deceive anyone, I want to emphasize that being charismatic is undoubtedly a great trait and tremendous asset to your soft skills. I don't want anyone reading this to think otherwise. If someone tries to conflate your charisma with being a little too smooth and call you out as a "bullshitter," don't let them throw that negative blanket on you. If it's not true, correct them quickly. By disregarding your charisma, they're overlooking your uniqueness and the distinct qualities of your personality. To avoid being categorized as the "average" or worse still, a phony salesperson, you must find a way for them to recognize and appreciate you as a charismatic individual. The risk of allowing this negative label is an incorrect perception that will or could lead to a sales death sentence.

Being naturally charismatic is a gift and learning to become more charismatic is a skill that can be learned. However, neither scenario is worthy of any attention, if not done sincerely. Sincerity is the foundation. If you aren't naturally charismatic and simply use these suggestions and tips to try to start forcing your newfound attention on to people, more than likely you won't achieve the desired effect. If you lack charisma and have never been naturally charismatic, trying to force your newly established charisma on people comes at a risk. Be careful. Attempting to be charismatic as I'm sure you can imagine, would look worse than not being charismatic at all. It's unbecoming to be seen as someone who's trying too hard and coming off as fake. Any behaviors that appear or even remotely appear to be contrived or insincere will not only backfire but will probably ensure you never get a second chance. You simply cannot, and will not, be or become charismatic if you do not genuinely believe in the goodness of being around people and engaging others.

Going hand in hand here, as previously discussed, is legitimate empathy so that when engaging with others, you further display sincerity and connectedness to them. It's tantamount for charismatic individuals to convey genuine interest and focus on those they're speaking with, regardless of any personal gain. You'll often find that charismatic people will do things for people they've just met or hardly know simply because they want to help. They want to inspire or energize someone to do, be or know something that will benefit the other person.

The warmth that real charismatic people have is difficult to fake. Quite often, people who are faking warmth or insincerely trying to appear genuine, are quickly discovered when their true motives appear. If you've never experienced this type of phoniness, it's quite disturbing and ugly. The classic example is the salesperson who lays it on thick for the purpose of closing a deal. Only revealing their true character once they recognize the sale or direction isn't going the way in which they want. Their real attitude and feelings quickly surface, and everyone is left a bit stunned during and after these phony sales encounters.

Recognize that all business meetings, transactions, and initial relationships are, in essence, based on what you can do for each other. It's tit for tat and assumed and commonplace to the dynamic. When I emphasize using your charisma, I mean specifically in its true and sincere definition. It's expected you would use your charisma to influence a person or group of people, however, please understand that if you approach life as a quid pro quo because of your charisma, you'll quickly lose your credibility. If charming to influence someone is always done for some personal or professional gain, then you'll in fact be displaying a personality that can be interpreted as a narcissist. Put another way, your only motive can't be giving to get! If you don't have a genuine desire to be around and engage with others out of social interest and curiosity, the phony risk is never worth the return. Meeting and getting to know others is worthy of your time and attention. If the attention and effort is directed solely to your end, prepare to lose opportunities, friends and more. In summary, yes indeed, some narcissists display charisma, but not all charismatic people are narcissistic. Never believe that being charismatic in the true definition is anything other than a positively wonderful and critical soft skill.

Don't always give to get.
Be comfortable just giving.

To be or not to be - a salesperson. This is the moment of truth, and I can't skate around it. If you don't like people, if you sincerely are not a people person, you simply will never attain significant success in sales within most sales roles. Of course, broken watches are right twice a day, yet, the very best salespeople are overwhelmingly gregarious, charismatic, extroverts and thrive in and amongst all types of people. In general, they prefer socialization to private time. They are driven to give and receive positivity through their interpersonal skills and socialization. This is not by accident.

You don't have to be the life of the party. You don't have to be the most charismatic person in the room to be successful in sales. However, you must be someone that is comfortable and happy to be interacting regularly with people of all types. If this isn't part of your DNA by the time you read this book, I gotta point out that you most likely won't have the success in your sales career that your peers who possess this trait will. I hate to use absolutes and discourage anyone new to the profession but now is the time to consider or reconsider your career choice.

My former boss once pleasantly caught me off guard by having a beer with me following a client visit. He complimented me on my ability to connect with our client and how quickly it appeared the client was opening up to us during our meeting. He continued to say that based on all his years in sales and sales leadership how critical he felt the skill of relationship building was for a successful salesperson. In a moment of disbelief, he added that building relationships was an area he had long wished he was stronger in and that he was envious of what he had seen during our meeting. Maybe you've heard what he told me next, but I never had, and it's stuck with me since. He told me most people don't understand the decision-making process when companies select vendors for their products or services. The average person will say it's the cheapest, or it's the one with the best product, or the best answer for the client's needs. Not actually true, he continued. Once you've been around long enough, you'll realize that buyers, stakeholders, and companies overwhelmingly make their purchasing decisions based on their sales rep first, the company's position or reputation next, and the solution last. Think about this, as it took me a moment to process. The solution or product last. He thought nothing about it at the time he delivered the statement. I've often brought it up to him since and told him what a succinct and perfect way his words were in my philosophy of the importance of soft skills. He was quick to point out that he wasn't the originator of this statement but, nonetheless; I let him know he'd always get credit in my book (thank you Wes).

One on my goals here is to illustrate this point through analyzing the soft skills that make a rep the most valuable part of a sale. This idea boils down to the individual sales rep's ability to earn trust and develop a sincere relationship with the client to ultimately win over an account. This could be the sole decision maker or a team of people within a company that, based on the sales rep's soft skills, gives him/her preferential treatment and the advantage of earning or renewing business. You might have a better solution or idea, you may work for a larger more established company, however, if I have earned the trust and am better liked than you, more times than not, I'll be awarded the business.

Are you struggling with the idea that someone would select doing business with a specific rep when a competitor has a better solution? Why would they? Because of the relationship, trust, and likability, haven't you been reading?! How does this work? Well, it typically goes something like this: Competitor A (B, C or D) reveals or demonstrates the best solution to the Decision Maker. The Competitor leaves and the Decision Maker calls the Salesperson that he/she likes the best and presents the Competitor's solution, giving their favorite Rep the opportunity to provide a similar option/service, etc. Sometimes this is referred to as "last look," while some folks (often on the losing side) of a bid call it bullshit favoritism. Call it whatever you will, but IT AIN'T GOIN' NOWHERE.

For those of you battling with this concept, I suggest researching how our brains make decisions. It comes as a surprise to most of us that we ultimately make our decisions based on emotion not logic. Soft skills appeal to the emotional side of our brains and connections with others. I'm not suggesting that I'm going to be given the contract to sell chemotherapy drugs to a hospital when I work for a tobacco manufacturer solely because they love me. Of course not. Remember, decision makers purchase in order of their relationship with a specific individual rep, the company's industry reputation and finally the solution presented. What makes the individual salesperson the first and primary consideration? Their mastery of soft skills and all they encompass. This is the whole shebang folks.

When dealing with people, remember you are not dealing with creatures of logic, but creatures of emotion.
—Dale Carnegie

First impressions are the impressions you must master. First impressions are kind of the only impression. Charismatic individuals never cease to leave positive, and often unique, first impressions. You've undoubtedly read, heard, or repeated the quote "You never get a second chance to make a first impression." 100% truth. There is no second place in first impressions. In Malcolm Gladwell's book Blink, we learn that in the first one-tenth to 60 seconds of meeting someone we make big assumptions about their character and how much we're going to like them, trust them, and believe them. He points out that studies have proven that these quick, first impressions we make are often validated and confirmed later down the road. Tolstoy's quote, "In difficult circumstances always act on first impressions," further illustrates how significant they are. While it seems obvious to me that it's impossible to define someone's entire character from a first impression, the research surrounding our intuition regarding others happens immediately, near instantaneously. It is because of this fact that ensuring that you nail your first impression is critical.

Two things remain irretrievable: time and a first impression.
—Cynthia Ozick

There's a fine line between phoniness and paying extra attention to ensure you leave a positive first impression. Ideally, you put energy into every single time you meet someone new, regardless of how they can help you in your professional life. If this isn't something do-able, then you absolutely must figure out a way to be "on" when you're first meeting anyone in your professional arena. I suggest you work on re-wiring your attitude and put in effort to make a very big (charismatic) first impression. Sincerely charismatic types leave positive, warm, and memorable first impressions on almost everyone they meet. They just do, it's natural or it's been learned, practiced, and become a part of their soft skills.

It is far easier to make a good first impression than it is to change a bad one.
—Michelle Tillis Lederman

Most of the time, people are so focused on being cool or charming and on making a strong first impression that they fail to show genuine interest in the other person with whom they're engaged. Their minds are working double time to say and do everything correctly, uniquely "cool-like," etc., when simply being interested, genuinely interested, in those you meet is the more important effort. People are overtaken with attraction and likability towards others when they ask sincere questions and show sincere interest about what they are interested in. This just works. Every single time. I'll get into listening skills shortly, but if you're a sincere, interested, and curious listener to people, they'll remember your face at the very least, and your face and name, at the very best.

What follows are some suggestions on how you can increase your charm and quickly draw people to you. Some of these suggestions done with sincerity and correctly will leave people directly understanding why they "like you." Others will leave them with that common, "Man, I really liked that person. I don't know why, I just really liked 'em…"

Below is something I've done for many years, and I believe some of you may have too. I want to share this tip because it's incredibly effective in quickly connecting with people. It's a safe bet I'm not the first with this tactic, but I've met enough people that were excited about the idea that I felt I should cover it just in case. Look at the three images below. Notice the name and note in brackets.

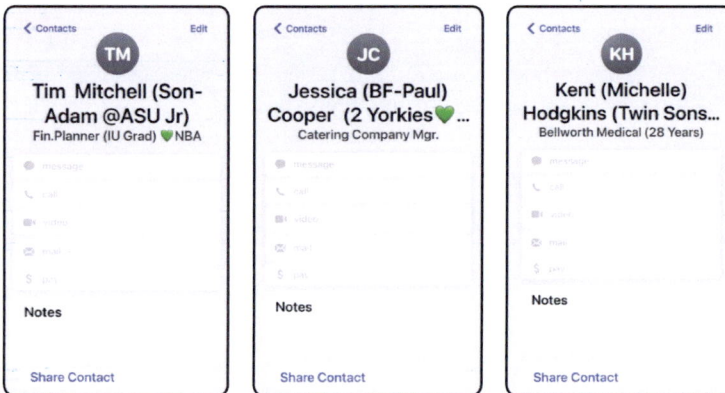

When you meet someone and are engaged in conversation, usually at some point, they'll reveal something of importance either personally or professionally. If (and when) they reveal this information such as the name of their significant other, the names and ages of their children, pets, or whatever professional accomplishment they've had, you've got to remember these things! Find a way you can capture and retain this information. Many times, I'll hold on to these names by repeating them in my mind (at the expense of active listening) as soon as I can, and I make notes on my phone. I can't think of a better or faster way to ingratiate yourself quickly with someone and start developing a legitimate relationship than by being able to recall their spouses, kids, or pets' names on your very next call. If a spouse or children are not named, you can literally note anything next to their name in your phone. Of course, the assumption is you've also asked for their mobile, or you've received their contact information. The trick is to put that important information in brackets next to their name so that when you call them, or if they call you, it pops up on your screen and you instantly are reminded of the person(s)/thing(s) that are of most importance or at least, something they're passionate about. Once you reconnect with the client, the fact that you remembered this piece of info or name(s), will instantly score big points in the likability area. There are lots of ways to quickly win people over, remembering names of those most important to them makes you likable, both consciously and subconsciously.

Giving someone a nickname quickly after meeting them is called a psychological trick. You can use it to build rapport quickly with almost anyone. For example, funny nicknames make people laugh and deepen connections by adding a sense of familiarity. As fake as it may sound, I've known a few people who make up a nickname midway or towards the end of first meeting someone (I've been the recipient of this also). Using someone's initials or a play on their initials is also a safe bet and a good way to connect quickly. Each repetition of a nickname or initials will bring a smile to their face and remind them that you have a funny, unique, and more than an initial surface level relationship developing. Delivered the right way, this does have a positive and impactful effect and can help connect you to someone quickly. Make one up and use it consistently to remind them you're becoming more familiar each time.

Confidence (not arrogance) is contagious; it gives an aura and draws others to you. This is often the first sign of a charismatic individual. They display a confidence that signals they're in control of everything they're saying and doing and are completely comfortable. Their confidence is often inspiring, and they have an ability to inspire those around them to become more confident and believe in themselves. Confidence is a major contributor to appearing and being charismatic. In order to be your most confident self, adhere to the keypoints below:

⇨ Be prepared.
⇨ Know your product/service – benefits and differentiators.
⇨ Ask questions – don't assume.
⇨ Know and believe in your personal and professional value.
⇨ Know your ideal and hard deck scenarios.
⇨ Ask for what you want – be ready to negotiate.
⇨ Be prepared to walk away respectfully and leave the door open.

In brief, being prepared and putting in the work beforehand, going in with a clear understanding of your company's product/service and differentiators, and finally, remaining detached from the outcome equals confidence. Detachment in this case means that whether the sale goes your way or not, it simply doesn't matter. Sometimes you'll hear the phrase sit back, so they'll lean in. This can be very difficult if a sales meeting has extra importance due to its potential to make you a large commission, or if you're under pressure from your manager to perform. I recently heard someone call this overt display of wanting (or needing) the sale as "commission breath." The salesperson who comes off too pushy or desperate comes to mind with this phrase. I don't know who gets credit for it, but whoever they are, it hit me in my funny bone with a sledgehammer. Either way, any display of being too eager or desperate will hurt you. Should you find yourself in either of these two situations, try closing your eyes before you go into the meeting and tell yourself, the less you need them, the more they'll want you. Repeat this several times.

Dale Carnegie famously wrote you should repeat a person's name three times within the first three minutes of meeting someone. Not sure this one is even debated as it's been the gold standard for decades. The human brain reacts strongly to the sound of its own name. It's often said that the sweetest sound to our ears is the sound of our own name. It grabs our attention, awakens our senses, and encourages us to listen closely. It truly does. I've been on the receiving end of a few salespeople who made me feel as if they literally had just finished reading Carnegie's book 10 minutes before shaking my hand. Jason, Jason, Jason…This can backfire, just like any tip or suggestion when you're trying new things to draw people to you. Practice working on it with friends and family first. Avoid going overboard at your next networking event and immediately repeating people's names back to them in a rush to say their name at least three times in three minutes. Be cool, or practice being a little cool on this one. Stay loose.

When you first meet someone, avoid flashing a smile immediately after shaking their hand. Instead, try looking them in the eye for about two seconds while slowly and steadily letting a smile come over your face and through your eyes. This might take some practice, but it's not a difficult skill to master. This brief delay gives someone the feeling that your smile is genuine and specific to meeting them! Not just the typical smile that we give as we're taught to smile and at least appear happy when we walk in a room or meet anyone. Nothing wrong with being happy or someone who smiles often. This certainly brightens the world. The point here is if you can turn it down or off prior to approaching a new person you're going to meet, shake their hand while looking them in the eye and pause, and then give a slow crescendo-ing warm smile toward them as a distinct individual, man it packs a charismatic punch. I've heard this referred to as "flooding" your smile and that is a perfect description. This form of body language exhibits powerful confidence and instantaneous charm. It's a unique way to leave a new acquaintance with a positive encounter.

Charisma is a key soft skill for salespeople. I still believe that in general, most people are suspicious and distrustful of salespeople. Having charisma allows you to build trust while leaving a critical creative, positive, first impression. Work on how you stroll towards or approach others, shake a hand, "flood" your smile, slow your speech down and occasionally tilt your head.
When it comes to new and creative ways to meet someone for the first time, 1 + 1 = 5. The first impression can not only increase your chance of a door opening, but quite often, it can break it the fuck down. As with every single suggestion within this book, you need to develop your own style with how you deliver and use these suggestions.

Practical Application

• **Practice self-confidence.** Dress professionally comfortably and be aware of your "presence." How you walk into a room, stand while talking, use your hands, hold your head and shoulders, etc., all make big impressions. Don't think for a second that everyone who sees and or speaks with you isn't rapidly processing judgments, both consciously and subconsciously.
I recently read an article where the author noted a technique that I found

interesting. Each time you enter a doorway (internally or externally) pull your shoulders back as you cross through the threshold. This ensures that the first impression anyone sees from a physical perspective is one of confidence.

• **Be first!** Be the one who goes first. Introduce yourself first. Help a stranger first. Say hello first. Life rewards people who initiate, not wait!

The FIRST MAN gets the OYSTER.
The second man gets the SHELL.
—Andrew Carnegie

• **When you shake someone's hand, take your opposite hand, and enclose the handshake.** You've seen, done or been a recipient of this most likely. Using both of your hands to greet someone for an initial handshake is a very powerful and warm way to make a quick connection and positive impression.

• **Demonstrate your interest by putting your hand on someone's shoulder (softly and quickly) after they've stated something that you've connected with.** This could of course backfire if used incorrectly or at the wrong time (or simply with someone who isn't comfortable with a shoulder touch). However, I'm including it as I'm of the belief that the risk is worth the return when done correctly.

• **Be an active listener.** Use your body language to ensure that whoever is speaking knows you are on pace and tracking their thoughts. I read somewhere about a technique that someone termed the "flicker technique." This is when you close your eyes briefly while smiling or having a warm facial expression to show thoughtfulness. This also displays you're intrigued by their statement and as a bonus, demonstrates your confidence while actively listening.

• **Ask open-ended questions.** Ask specific questions that most people appreciate and will be interested in answering with more than a yes or no. Personal hobbies and interest questions are universally well received and get people talking. Asking what people are passionate about goes along these lines and of course, taking an interest in someone's children and getting them to talk about what's going on with them is a great runway for them to open up in order for you to connect.

• **Be positive.** A positive attitude is infectious and naturally attracts people. Focus on the positive of everything and never make a turn down negative street. Even if the other person starts turning the conversation negative, do all you can to drive both of you out of it and back to a positive mindset. Your display of staying positive has a direct and indirect power to attract people to you.

• **Smile, smile, and smile some more.** ☺

• **Use your voice to express your passion.** Pitch and tone convey enthusiasm and passion for whatever you're talking about. Use your vocal tools, they have a significant ability to showcase your charisma.

• **Be prepared for every meeting with your clients.** Do your research, have all you need ready and anticipate things you might want to bring just in case. Further, be ready to handle objections or questions. Think about what probable objections or questions may be coming so you can manage them effortlessly. The power of preparation when it comes to managing clients' challenges, objections, issues, or questions can win someone over very quickly. Remember, if it can go wrong or it's on your short list of worries, it most likely will go wrong. Prepare for it in advance!

• **Seek thrilling opportunities.** Oddly enough, I once read that elevating a person's heart rate as well as eating spicy foods forces our emotions into hyperactivity with nervousness, excitement, joy, and relief. Consider roller coasters and spicy food for initial meetings (just make sure they can take it). If you can find a way to entertain your clients with experiences that elevate their heart rate, it will help you have bonding experiences that last. These experiences can also be brought up, referenced, and drawn upon later to display once again familiarity and relationship growth.

• **Create an inside joke.** This produces a sense of exclusivity in your relationship and acts as a bonding agent. When you make an inside joke, suddenly, there are only very few people in the world who know what it's referring to. This generates a feeling of closeness and keeps the relationship bonded ■

Listen Hear!
Listening

You never really learn much from hearing yourself speak.

—George Clooney

I spent 365 days (to the day) in Japan beginning in 1997. I took an educational sabbatical from the San Diego County Probation Department; and off I went as a first time 27-year-old conversational English teacher on a small island off the mainland. For reference, I was south of Nagasaki a few hours by car and a long way from Tokyo. What made this one of the most significant and beautiful years of my life is that the city I lived in, Hondo City, was small, rural, and very traditional. I was, to my knowledge, only one of two Americans living in the city during this time out of approximately 55,000 inhabitants. So, yeah, you could say I stood out a bit. I believe the residents preferred it that way too. No matter where I went, the people made what seemed to me a big deal of my presence. They may not have liked me for whatever reason; however, they NEVER made me feel anything less than respected, welcomed, and appreciated for being in their city. I had a very, very small glimpse into what being a celebrity might feel like. No literary exaggeration here, the proverbial red carpet was laid out on several occasions for little old (well, younger then) me. The Japanese were the most beautiful of people and expressed nothing but kindness and respect every second I lived in their country. I truly miss everyone I met during my time in Japan. Looking back on this adventure is surreal, but I am eternally grateful that I fought back my fear and went for it. The only regret I have about the entire experience is that I didn't extend my time and stay for a second year. If you're Japanese or of Japanese descent and reading this book, I simply want to say thank you. Thank you for being part of a country and culture that made me see the world differently. Thank you for teaching me to appreciate that other places had equal, or in some cases, better things than I had at home. Also, for helping me realize the world is a great big place that I wish everyone could get an opportunity to experience.

While I was in Japan, I went to visit a group of teachers at a school for special education students. I had a translator and several of the school administrators and staff wanted to meet me and ask questions. All kinds of questions, but mostly to get to know me and my thoughts on Japan. This is where I observed and learned a very interesting and significant lesson in listening. Each time I would answer a question, it would be translated to the staff member who asked the question. I would watch the translator translate my response and the questioner receive the translation. What happened next, and continued to happen for the entirety of the time I was there, was remarkable. There would be a long pause before any replies in the Q&A. I mean, long pauses. Uncomfortably long pauses, the kind where you are wondering if the person is "all there." Sometimes, especially with the older gentlemen at the table, they would put their head down while pausing and then lift it when replying to the translator.

When we were done and driving back in the car, I asked my boss why the people took so long to answer and put their head down before replying. My boss replied that in Japan it was considered somewhat rude to reply too quickly during a conversation or worst still, to speak over someone. The long pause was a display of respect while listening and contemplating what I had just said. The pause was there so that the listener could focus on my question or response and think about and process what they had just heard. The head dropping down was simply body language to accentuate respect for the speaker. My boss added, the Japanese feel that if you say something and someone instantly replies after you've just made a statement, that you couldn't have possibly listened and thought about what they said to prepare your best response. In comparison, two Americans engaged in a conversation might look like a machine gun of words and body language versus two Japanese speaking and pausing to think about their replies as if in slow motion. Pausing and waiting a couple seconds before replying in a conversation is a great way to avoid talking over someone and I highly recommend it (although I struggle still in this area). The Japanese can do this with ease and it's quite an interesting and impressive observation when new to their culture.

The biggest communication problem is we do not listen to understand. We listen to reply.
—Stephen R. Covey

Active listening not only helps you grasp both spoken and unspoken messages but also enhances your charisma and magnetism. We often hear someone say how great of a speaker someone is. However, we rarely hear someone say, "That gal or guy was a fantastic listener." Yet, when we meet with someone who is an active and "great" listener, we remember them. We rarely call out that skill, but just leave that encounter with a very positive impression. I think ya'll know what I'm talking about here. Take it even one step further and actively and sincerely listening is ultimately a show of respect for whoever you're communicating with. The Japanese are very proud people with a culture that stresses being respectful, possibly more so than any other culture in the world. It was impressive and very interesting to observe during my time. Many years later, I returned to Japan with two good friends who were San Diego police officers. This trip was arranged by a good Japanese friend and former roommate who wanted to take the three of us to a meet and greet with his network. He was starting a bodyguard-security type of business in Japan where he would arrange Japanese tourists and/or students wanting to travel to the United States. His plan was to coordinate and arrange off-duty

American law enforcement officers to lead tours and essentially be drivers for Japanese tourists to ensure they were safe for whatever or wherever they wanted to see and go. His business plan was that his clients would be getting a bodyguard and tour guide all in one. Sadly, the Japanese then (and I'd bet still now) are very interested in visiting the U.S., but they're generally quite frightened due to our cultural violence.

What happened upon our arrival was a complete and remarkable surprise that I'll never forget. My Japanese friend helped us check in to our hotel and pulled me aside in the lobby. He proceeded to tell me that we're going to be picked up for dinner by some friends of his friends that wanted to meet American law enforcement officers. I said, "That's great," and he then paused and asked if we would be uncomfortable spending a few hours at a restaurant with the local Yakuza boss. I had to ask him to repeat what he had just said as I wasn't sure if it was due to his elementary level of English, or I had just heard what I thought I heard. He laughed and told me that there would be absolutely no problems, no danger, and that it would be a favor to him. I checked in with my cop friends and they were ok with it, and we mostly thought it was going to be a couple guys overselling their relationship with some local Yakuza wannabes.

My friend had friends, who had friends, who were aligned with the Japanese mafia, better known as the Yakuza. If you're not familiar with the Yakuza, it's very much like most criminal organizations and operates many illegal activities. For those of you who have seen the film Black Rain, starring Michael Douglas and Andy Garcia, the events I'm about to share would have fit perfectly within this film. (Side note: if you haven't seen the movie, I highly recommend it; it's an outstanding cop vs. bad guys film.) Anyways, we got checked in to the hotel and because this story isn't odd enough, let me add that our bags didn't make it to Japan with our flight. So, we were given vouchers to go to the local mall and buy whatever we needed for 48 hours (the window in which we would receive our luggage). Imagine for a moment three American law enforcement guys, all former football players, shopping for clothing in Japan…Absolutely nothing fit a single one of us! The pants were three inches too short; shirts were two sizes too small. So yeah, we met in the lobby and looked like three clowns who didn't know how to dress. Not the way we wanted to start our trip (or meet with a group of Japanese mafia members).

While we were waiting, two gentlemen walked in all dressed in black and then escorted us out into a limousine. Once we got inside, there were two more men dressed in black who greeted us. We drove and arrived at the restaurant a short while later. We exited the limo and there were two more men, dressed in black, outside the entrance. We all filed in and were taken to a back room. We arrived at the doors to a private room. They were the paper type of sliding doors (shoji) that you see if you're familiar with Japanese restaurants and how they separate private rooms for larger parties. A staff member from the restaurant slid back the doors and inside was an older Japanese man (the local boss), his female translator, and two more men, yes, they too were dressed in black.

At this point, we were certain that whoever these people were, they were most certainly not pretending to be more than they were. Introductions were made and I was sat directly across from the boss. The big boss immediately started asking numerous questions about me, us, life in America, and our thoughts about Japan. The entire conversation was being quarterbacked by his female translator and going along nicely, pauses and all. None of us could believe the scene we were sitting in, and we were simply taking it in and playing it as if it were just another night out for dinner. My friend periodically leaned towards me repeating, "Jason-san, it's ok, no problems, this is safe and no danger." Of course, my friends were wondering what the hell I'd gotten us into. At no point did any of us believe we were not sitting in a room with an extremely high ranking, important Yakuza gang member (and yes, he was missing half of his pinky finger—for those of you who were wondering). After an hour or so of sincere and honest questions and pleasantries, the real reason for us having dinner revealed itself. The translator asked me if I, or any of my American law enforcement contacts, would be willing or able to ship over bullet-proof vests. I looked at my friends and we all smiled politely and respectfully, as I replied we couldn't help them. The dinner went on and we eventually were escorted back to the hotel with full stomachs, good buzzes, laughs, and a remarkable shared experience for all of us for the rest of our lives.

The reason I shared this story was to address active listening once again and use the Japanese as an example of how serious they take this aspect of communication. Here I was, sitting with a stranger for the better part of three hours, a stranger who was a high-ranking Japanese mafia member, engaged in a conversation (through a translator). From the moment we sat down, he was completely focused and engaged. He paused every time something was said to him via the translator, sometimes he would put his head down, other times not, and then he would look at me and reply. The cadence of pausing to think and reply was the same here, as it was with the school officials, I had met over a decade earlier. This man had no reason to show us any display of respect. He could have easily paid less attention and most certainly could have avoided focused pauses if he so desired.

Whether communicating with school officials, or a Yakuza boss, the Japanese active listening culture is remarkable. You can't help but leave a conversation feeling heard, understood, and respected. These are ideal feelings that anyone wants finishing a sales meeting or personal conversation. Successful active listening takes energy and focus but the return on your investment will make a lasting impact. You'll see that you take away more from each conversation, you'll make fewer comprehension mistakes, and you'll connect with whoever you are engaged with as an active listener in ways that will immediately build trust and strengthen a relationship.

As I was putting this together and having my wife assist in the review, she insisted I realize that my listening skills as a professional have been perfected for the purpose of my success. She was quick to point out, and I must admit, that my listening skills when it comes to her speaking about us personally, are of a much less polished and prioritized nature. She's got me there. I know how to listen when it comes to sales, however, I've struggled with listening to my wife about her, me, us, the kids, you know, all those things that are the most important to us as humans! If you can master listening for both personal and professional purposes, well friends–you have just ensured a happy wife, happy life combo. Congrats!

It's important to distinguish the difference between hearing and listening. Hearing is involuntary and passive. Hearing is the process of sound reaching our ears, and this occurs whether we want it or not. Listening is voluntary and active. Listening is the process of actively paying attention to what is being said or heard. It takes hearing to its most focused level so that we can under-stand and interpret what is being communicated.

Decades back, I remember reading an article entitled something like We Hear What We Listen For…. Essentially, it was an article addressing our decreasing attention spans and how we are hearing but not listening enough to others (see my wife's previous thoughts on my personal listening skills). We're simply going through the communication motions until something strikes us as different, unique or of personal interest and importance. We can tune anyone or anything out that we want and often do this subconsciously. We can choose to hear only what we wish to listen to. The author of the article asked the reader to imagine walking down a busy Manhattan sidewalk during lunch hour. People all around you talking. None of the other individuals' conversations are registering, dozens of people are speaking simultaneously and loudly! You couldn't recall a single conversation aside from the one you were having with your coworker, maybe. However, out of nowhere, someone drops a pocket full of change and instantly everyone turns to look and see what and where! How in the hell did you hear the sound? There's so much noise, direct conversation, chatter all around, laughing, yelling, taxis, police sirens, music, and you pinpointed the sound of a handful of change falling to the ground. Everyone within earshot immediately changes focus from who they were talking with to the sound of money crashing to the sidewalk. I thought it was a powerful and glaring statement about us hearing what we listen for, or in this example, what is of primary importance to us.

Leaning in and paying sincere attention is one of the best skills we can possess. Active listening also displays a soft skill that is often overlooked and under-appreciated. Most people accept that others are only half listening or pretending to be listening, because that's what most of us do! When you can show someone that you're completely invested in what they're saying, you ingratiate them quickly. Often, they leave a meeting or conversation not even knowing exactly why they were drawn to you. The fact is, you were actively listening, so they felt a range of emotions from being genuinely valued to important. All of which are universally appreciated.

Many of us are becoming more accustomed to multi-tasking. Not just in the traditional physical sense of the term, but even worse, during our thought processes. We can be listening to someone and instantly something creeps into our mind that we're supposed to be doing next or that is of greater importance. I heard the comedian George Carlin say something to the effect of although we're more technologically advanced and efficient; we have less time and focus. This is sad, but very true. (George was so very ahead of his time). Whichever way you consider multi-tasking, it's important to understand that science has proven it doesn't work. Neuroscientists have calculated that multitasking slows productivity by 50% and increases mistakes by 50%. We get half as much done, remarkable in and of itself, and significantly increase our errors! The risk isn't worth the reality if we acknowledge the science. Not only does it decrease productivity, increase the risk of mistakes and bad decisions, but it also makes us less creative. Yet, how many of us still engage in it day after day?

Deciding to listen is an intentional and purposeful gesture. It's for this reason that when you actively listen and are sincerely curious when having a conversation with others, they gravitate towards you, either consciously or subconsciously. Active, focused listening displays a special recognition and respect that is simply and sadly rare. Why rare? Because it's utterly exhausting to listen with focus and purpose. Do you know why the word "exhausting" caught your eye and stood out in that last sentence? Because we usually don't actively listen for that very reason, it's entirely exhausting. We often underestimate the power of true listening. We're so bombarded with imagery and sounds marketed to take up so much space in our minds that we're paying less and less attention to others when they're speaking. The space that is taken up in our brain by social media, 24-hour news cycles, and all the normal daily information we receive from our lives, combined with the speed in which we receive information, is literally burning us out. So, to those rare individuals who can actively listen and recognize the effort and concentration required to be truly memorable, I applaud you! This knowledge and skill are grossly underrated and undervalued.

Because I'm hopeful that current and future salespeople are reading this book, I should make the quick connection to actively listening and its importance to the sales process. You've undoubtedly heard or read things like, "God gave us two ears, two eyes, and one mouth so we could listen and observe more than we speak." Or "Listen more than you speak during a sales meeting." There are many unique quotes like this flying around left over from previous decades and new versions of the same sentiment coming out all the time. They all say the same thing. Shut the fuck up and listen. Your buyer, your decision maker, your stakeholder, whomever you have in front of you is the person you want talking. You want to ask open-ended questions and learn how to lead your meetings into conversations that get your person talking so that you can listen and learn. If you're asking good questions and actively listening, chances are good that you'll hear the answers that you need to earn, make, and close your sale.

If you're like most salespeople, you likely speak very well. You're able to articulate your message with energy and confidence and perhaps with charisma. These are necessary skills. However, there's a good chance you're not even aware of how often you talk more than you listen during your meetings. Try this exercise. The very next sales presentation or meeting you have with a first client (first being the key) where you can be accompanied by a teammate or colleague, ask him or her to tally (approximately or exactly) your time speaking versus listening to the client. I think you'll be surprised at the imbalance. The treasure received from any sales meeting is produced by your target and takes only your ability to ask good questions and actively listen.

Know how to listen and you will profit from even those who talk badly.
—Plutarch

Bruce Lee famously stated, "Most people can talk without listening, very few can listen without talking." He nailed it, as he did with so many things in his life. The difference is the ability to remain still and silent although every piston in your brain is begging your mouth to talk. Our brains are complex and more cluttered than ever. We're taking in new information at a rate never seen nor anticipated. I recall a story about what a neurologist had told a friend of mine. He (the doc) said that he and the entire medical community are seeing an astronomical increase in patients complaining about memory loss and related issues. His opinion and feeling at the time (about five years back) was that our minds are being bombarded with new information from every single angle, every single minute. He stated that he believed we were not meant to process and take in the new volume of daily information and that we were/are at the beginning of a neurological evolution. Our brains are going to have to take a couple steps backward, before they evolve to the new norm of social media, 24-hour news channels, and every other form of constant entertainment, news, or educational stream we're continuously bombarded with every day. We expect leaders and influential individuals (salespeople) to be brilliant speakers. Those natural born, more charismatic people are rewarded most of their life for having the "gift of gab." This very book is a testament to its power. Ironically, the gift of being an active and passionate listener is rarely respected unlike those who have a way with words that are positively mesmerizing.

We have two ears and one mouth so we can listen more than we speak.
—Epictetus

Practical Application

• **Periodic paraphrasing.** Every so often, pause during conversations and paraphrase back to the speaker what you've heard. Bonus, try using similes, metaphors or an anecdote that matches exactly what they're expressing, and you'll see (almost literally) a light bulb go off on their face. The sender's body language will scream out, "Yes, you get me!"

• **Let your face do the talking.** Give your speaker facial cues that you're listening, interested and focused. Smile, frown, and display facial gestures that are synced with the emotion of either your speaker or the events being spoken.

• **Follow the Japanese rule:** Wait two seconds before speaking when engaged in a conversation. This helps you learn to avoid interrupting and speaking over someone. It also displays a confident, calm, and engaged cadence that displays maturity and intellectual strength (even more benefits to lasting impressions).

• **Focus to stay present in the moment.** Try to clear your mind and fully concentrate on the person speaking. When your mind wanders (and it will) redirect your focus back to the speaker.

• **Remember personal or professional details about others.** This is an excellent way to build trust. Remembering key details impresses your speaker as well as subconsciously tells the speaker that you're interested and engaged. It never fails and you've probably heard someone say, "How'd you remember that?" If you should ever hear this phrase, know that you've just scored a significant point in your relationship-building process.

Let Your Face Do The Talking
Communication

Because of what is said and not meant, and what is meant and not said, most of love is lost.

—Kahlil Gibran

Because of what is said and not meant, and what is meant and not said, most of COMMUNICATION is lost.

—Kahlil Gibran with a twist

I can think of very few problems in my past that didn't revolve wholly or primarily around poor communication. My inability to articulate the best way at a particular moment, or another person I was engaged with failing to communicate effectively are at the root of many problems. Assumption isn't the mother of all fuck ups, poor communication is. After all, assuming is a poor form of communication. While assuming can backfire and have negative consequences, it doesn't always hurt us. Yet, poor communication has, does, and always will create severe business and personal failures.

What have you done to improve your ability to communicate effectively and be a better listener? I'm guessing nothing, the same for most of us. We take a speech class or two through our formal educational avenues. Any courses on how to listen actively and effectively? Regrettably, in our public education system, we're not taught listening skills as a critical component of communication. Therefore, it's the responsibility of individuals seeking to improve their professional and personal lives to actively work on enhancing their listening skills and to improve their overall communication. The results of improving your communication will last forever and advance your goals in ways you never knew existed.

Let's look at a breakdown of communication. Depending on what study, or which author you read, communication is approximately 60% what we see, 20-30% how we say and hear things (the vocal elements of volume, articulation, etc.) and only 10-20% are the actual words that come out of our mouths. The significance of body language doesn't surprise most of us, however, when you look at the overwhelmingly dominant emphasis it has on the totality of our communication, it's startling. What we see is more than half the message being communicated. Over half. No words, no sounds. Over half! I don't believe most salespeople truly understand or appreciate this breakdown and emphasis on the visual element of communication. If you are new or newer to sales, I implore you to trust the studies and breakdown of visual, vocal, and verbal elements regarding communication, both sent and received. Your facial expressions, your hand gestures, your posture, the clothes you wear and all the physical attributes on and about you send the largest and strongest message of your communication. Perception is reality!

I gotta teach my facial expressions how to use their inside voices.
—Author Unknown

Consider an additional 20-30% of how we communicate is vocal. This is the message conveyed through our vocal tone and inflection. What does that leave us for the actual words that come out of our mouth when we communicate? 10-20%! Just think about this for a moment. Pause and really think about this. When you communicate, the words spoken carry the least impact, emphasis, and importance in the overall communication process.

Look no further than texting someone. How many times have you written or received a text and felt an emotion that was not intended? My guess is that most of us who text regularly, both professionally and personally, have experienced this many times. The reason is simple. We have no visual or vocal experience during this form of communication. We've hacked off about 80% of the most important ways we communicate! However, we expect that texting gets our message across clearly and succinctly. This is very counterintuitive indeed. Emojis were invented for this very reason. Let's come up with symbols that we can quickly add to our text so that our reader understands the emotion we're conveying. Let's make no mistake about it and add in that happy face. Again, if you've texted as much as most people in this electronic device era, even the use of an emoji doesn't necessarily give us the same confirmation of a communicated message. Why? Because we're missing the other ingredient of communication. We're missing the vocal part. We can't hear the tone or inflection and we ultimately can't combine the three forms of communication together. Effective communication absolutely requires harmony between the visual, vocal, and verbal components.

A whopping 10-20% of communication is done with the actual words that come out of our mouth. This percentage is startling to most people who learn this for the first time. If you simply look at the percentage breakdown of the elements of communication, it's incredible that the words spoken carry the least importance. However, if you're a student of communication and understand how critical the body language (non-verbal) and vocal cues are to our messaging, it becomes easier to grasp.

It's simply not enough to be cognizant of how important body language and your voice are in communicating. We must understand that all three forms of communication need to work with each other to give us the best chance of success in sending or receiving our messages. For example, if someone for some strange reason were to appear very depressed and have a severely somber tone while congratulating you on your bonus, you would be left wondering if you'd just heard what you thought you heard. Your reaction would be dubious to be sure. Your mind would be wondering, "Wait, did I just get a bonus? But the person looked sad and lethargic…" Huh? If there's any confusion in our sending of a message to someone, the listener will always recall the visual part of the message. Why? Why wouldn't they when 50% or more of our communication is done visually through body language and other nonverbal communication?

Another example, if I introduce myself in a conference room and hold up my hand proudly with three fingers displayed to show that I've worked for a company for five years, you know what they'll remember when they leave my meeting? What my hand showed them. NOT what I said to them, but what they saw. They'll leave believing I've worked on the job for three years (what my hand signaled), not the actual five years that came out of my mouth. Understanding these basics of communication is important in developing the best habits possible for effectively communicating. Understanding the elements of communication allows us to focus on the things we're doing to ensure our best chance of delivering our messages the way in which we wish them to be received. Having knowledge of how all communication is sent and received benefits us in all aspects of communication. You want to increase your likability sincerely and quickly, then learn to communicate most effectively. Watch how fast all your other soft skills skyrocket once you improve your communication skills.

I'd let myself down if I didn't point out in this chapter that WORDS MATTER. In fact, they matter second only to our actual character and actions. Now I know what you're thinking. I just wrote a couple pages back that only 10-20% of communication involves the actual words that we speak. Yes, yes, that is true. However, recall that all three elements are critical and must work together in harmony to send the message. Words are statistically the least important component in communicating messages, both sent and received. But they're NOT mutually exclusive from our personality and character. Just because they carry the least statistical weight doesn't excuse the speaker from his or her responsibility to their meaning and definitions. Words are and always have been connected to who we are and how we are judged and seen. If we speak it, we are it. Try making a controversial statement sometime and then saying, "I was just kidding and didn't mean it." We know how this works and it ultimately leaves a poor taste in our listeners'/readers'/observers' mouths.

When we discuss good communication, we generally use the phrase effective communication. You simply will not be successful in sales (or in life) without being able to effectively communicate. The ability to express yourself and listen to others will help you build trust quickly. You already know that trust is the foundation of successful relationship building. Effective communication involves active listening and expressing empathy which will help solidify your client relationships. When clients recognize you understand their needs, they quickly begin to trust you. Trust provides you with the pathway to grow your business and relationship. Notice the connection between communication to the other soft skills.

No salesperson will be their best if they don't understand the discovery element to the sales process. Discovery is where we ask questions during meetings to ensure we understand our clients' needs. The more effective communicator you are, the better able you are to ask the right questions to identify their needs. The goal is always the same and never changes. Identify the prospect's needs so that you can communicate your tailored solutions that will solve their need (problems)–bullseye. The better you can communicate, the easier it will be to articulate your added value so you can separate yourself from the competition.

You can see the significant benefits of effective communication but wait, there's more! More benefit to you professionally and personally. When you communicate effectively, you're more likely to be successful no matter what your position. As previously mentioned, you're able to establish trust and build stronger bonds through effective communication. You'll also help create or contribute to the overall health of your team environment. Positive team environments within any company bring out the collective best in any organization.

Being able to effectively communicate helps you control your emotions. Not sure if you've ever lost your shit at your job or the professional arena but believe me when I tell you... no good comes of it. When you're able to productively express your feelings and disruptive issues, you'll find that you have significantly less stress. This will be a major contributing factor to your work-life balance. If you think the phrase "work-life balance" isn't serious, you're either too young to understand it or too out of balance to come out of it.

Picture you're in a sales meeting or any personal conversation and suddenly something emotionally charges the person you're engaging. The examples are endless because most of us struggle to control our emotions. We're an emotional group of folks here in the United States. Culturally, we're prone to fighting back and speaking our mind to whoever, whenever and wherever. My cousin once told me a story where he "got into it" with someone. He finished the story with, "Hey, don't light the fuse if you don't wanna hear the bang!" I thought that was brilliant, and I quickly agreed with him on this point. What he was saying is that you shouldn't fuck around and push a topic when you notice someone is becoming emotionally charged. Ok, noted. This is great when close family or friends are ranting about a person or event in private. However, when you meet with a potential client/prospect and you notice something you've said emotionally charges your counterpart, you've got to shut it down quickly. Same goes for if someone you're meeting with hits your emotional button(s) subtlety or with a sledgehammer. Lock it up and control it!

Let me quickly address the most common barriers to effective communication: personal, psychological, semantic, organizational, and cultural. First, personal barriers. Personal barriers include fears of challenging authority, an unwillingness to communicate or open up, and/or not having incentive to speak your mind. Second, psychological barriers. Ego, ego, ego. Did I mention ego? They're also present because of previous events, which we commonly refer to as being "snake bitten" by someone or something formerly. These examples contribute to our moods, attitudes, and relationships. Next, semantic barriers. Semantic barriers include word choice and formal and informal slang or catch phrases, which can have varied cognitive meaning and risk not being understood equally. Organizational barriers are also a barrier to communication. These include the status of others, the complexity in the organization chart, and physical locations. Finally, cultural barriers. The diversity and culture of the culture in the workplace can have a dramatic impact on communication.

Make sure your communication is clear and that your speaking is easily understood. Be concise, the more words you use, the more opportunity for confusion, misunderstanding, or losing someone's attention. Lastly, be correct in the information that you're sharing, relying upon, or referring to. If your facts are incorrect, you'll not only screw up the message, but you're also risking escalating a conflict that may have not been there previously.

An excellent suggestion for effective communication: Ask questions! Get people talking about what is important to them and what they're passionate about and don't just hear, but actively listen. However, you do it, lock in and leave no doubt to your speaker that they have your full attention. Paraphrase back at points to not only ensure you're tracking, but to routinely remind your speaker that YOU ARE LISTENING and remembering.

Avoid the poor habit that many people use during communication that happens like this: you're telling a story or giving an example of something you've done, went through or experienced and your listener's very first reply to your thoughts is, "That happened to me and let me tell you…" or "My neighbor had that happen and she went to the hospital…." People mistakenly fall into the habit of following up your story with their similar experience and it often feels like they're trying to win a contest. Worse, you can't help but think, consciously or subconsciously, that they weren't really listening as they showed no empathy before launching right into their similar but always more impactful, serious, stressful, tragic story.

Here's a sample dialogue that may sound familiar: "I'm exhausted but feeling better. It's been three weeks since I was diagnosed. I'm Covid free, but just feeling down and depressed. I lost so much momentum in both my professional and personal life." Before you finish this breath or 1/100th of a second after you complete your thought, your friend replies, "When I had Covid, I didn't leave bed for 14 days and that was after I was admitted to the hospital for three days. I know what ya mean, I lost a big account from being out." How could they possibly express sincere empathy? Did they even listen to the entirety of your thoughts? This is an example of someone trying to reply that they've had it harder, worse, or more challenging and is unfortunately far too often the norm in conversation. If you want to improve your communication, if you want to sincerely make someone feel heard, then you'll stop doing this or at least begin to recognize this isn't ideal communication.

Here's how it would look for a sincerely considerate and aware person in this conversation. "I'm exhausted but feeling better. It's been three weeks since I was diagnosed. I'm Covid free, but just feeling down and depressed. I lost so much momentum in both my professional and personal life." This would be the much better reply: "I'm so sorry to hear that. I remember when we spoke a few days following your diagnosis, how horrible you sounded on the telephone. I can only imagine how frustrating and depressing that was for you not being able to get out of bed or do anything productive. Did you lose your sense of hearing or taste? I heard that has happened to a lot of people who've had Covid. What do ya mean you lost some things at work and personally? Tell me about that." You could wrap this by ending with, "…for whatever it's worth, you were missed around here at the office as well as at our weekly Friday happy hours. Welcome back!" Night and day differences here, as well as perceptions and appreciation from the person you're speaking with.

I was talking with a close friend of mine one day and he expressed how he's stopped sharing any significant things going on with his kids with most of our other friends. When I asked him why he replied, "I just find myself increasingly disappointed in how little sincerity or attention is given back to me after I've wholeheartedly and energetically asked about their kids." My friend felt as if he was sincerely and actively asking about our friends' kids and when the conversation got to our friends asking about his kids, he never felt the interest and listening given back to him was genuine. The expected/hoped for social listening reciprocity was minimal, insincere, or simply nonexistent. There is a type of friendship conversational norm, or our conditioned social obligation at minimum, in friendly conversation in that "you ask, I ask" type of way.

I can't say that I haven't felt this way personally before and this speaks to our communication norm in society. We're moving in different directions and have more on our minds than ever before. We go through the communicative motions and say just enough to show we're not selfish or disconnected from those we're engaged with. We tend to stay at the minimally expected level of conversation. For this reason, we have an excellent opportunity professionally and personally to slap someone in their mind and wake 'em' up!

What I mean is by behaving differently (in this case displaying more sincerity and actively showing more interest, even slightly more) to the average person, first meet or longtime friend, it's interpreted in their mind as remarkable and significant. We've become accustomed to "Hey how ya doing...?" and then our minds go on autopilot, almost canned or pre-scripted responses take over dialogue. Not just responses, but also in our body language and tone. Put it all together and to an outside observer and it would look like both parties are hardly engaged. As I mentioned in the chapter on listening, be present and attentive. Give your full attention when someone is speaking to you. Active listening is one of the best ways to win someone over.

The quality of your communication is the quality of your life.
— Tony Robbins

Practical Application

• **Be concise in all forms of your communication.** Avoid unnecessary information.

• **Use visual aids such as pictures, charts, or videos to help explain your ideas, service, or product.** Visual aids reinforce your message and do wonders to make your message memorable.

• **Speak clearly and minimize slang words that may not be picked up on by your listener.**

• **Be positive in speech, thought and manner.** Be mindful that positivity conveys confidence in your product or services.

• **Use examples and case studies.** They help illustrate your points and reinforce your message.

• **Be a great storyteller.** Arguably this is the most powerful way to communicate ideas, persuade clients, and build relationships. Practice structuring your stories so that they're pertinent while being entertaining. Stories can show how your products or services can help solve client's problems or make them better.

• **Recognize your listener's behavioral style and how they prefer to be communicated with.** A quick example is an extrovert attempting to communicate with an introvert. Be careful not to speak too aggressively to someone who is displaying a timid behavior style. Don't speak too informally if you notice your listener, is a formal speaker. Slow down if your listener speaks slowly. Speed up if your listener speaks quickly. Adapt your style to ensure that your target has the ideal chance to understand your message, which just so happens to be explaining your value.

• **Follow up with your client after a sale to ensure they're happy with your product or service.** You'd be shocked to know how rarely this happens in many sales cycles. Don't assume your client is satisfied with whatever you just sold them. Pick up the phone or go see them in person to make sure everything is exactly as they wanted and expected. This ingratiates a salesperson quickly and strongly. If you take nothing else from this chapter, communicate via a follow up call to ensure your client is completely satisfied.

E-Go I

**If you are irritated by every rub,
how will you be polished?**
—Rumi

GOT YA ☺

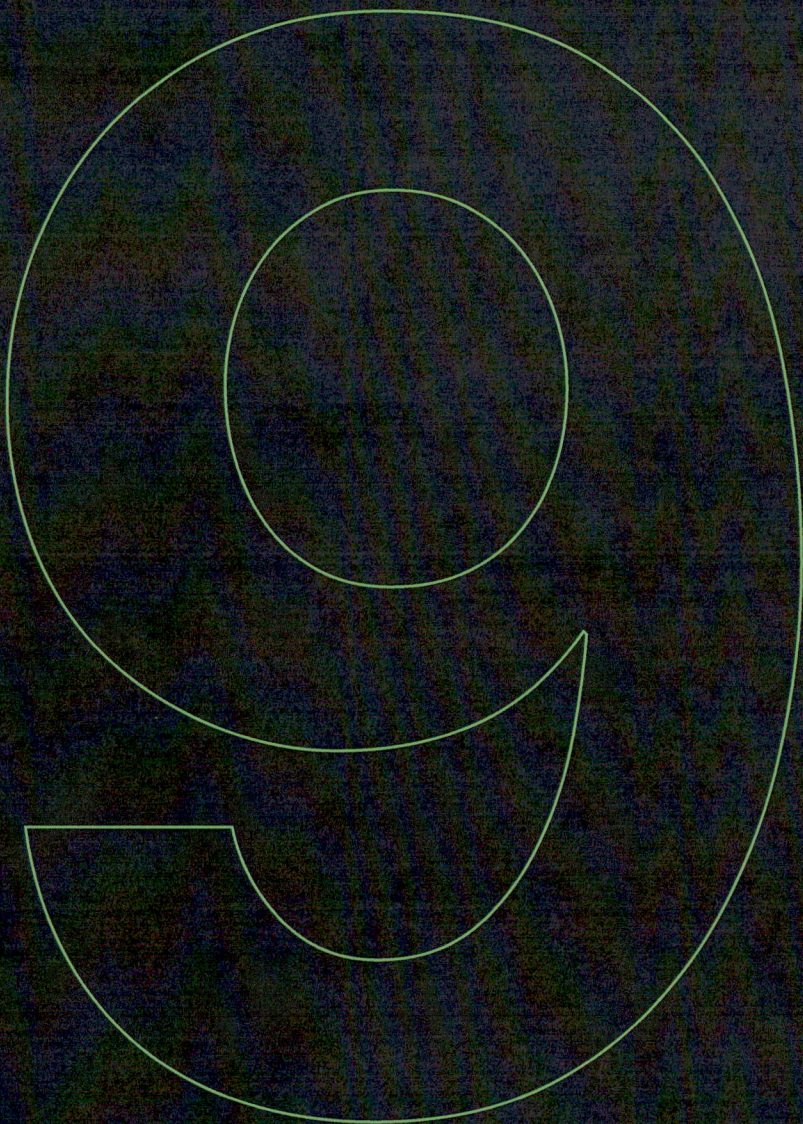

E–GO! II

Ego is the enemy–giving us wicked feedback, disconnected from reality. It's defensive, precisely when we cannot afford to be defensive. It blocks us from improving by telling us that we don't need to improve. Then we wonder why we don't get the results we want, why others are better and why their success is more lasting.

—Ryan Holiday, Ego is the Enemy

I was taking a shot at trying something different by purposefully leaving a couple pages blank on Ego I. I hope that you turned the pages wondering WTF happened. Was there a misprint by chance? Did I purchase a bad book? What the hell is going on? Perhaps it did the trick, maybe it didn't, but it was worth a try. Remember, try something. Try anything to be a little different in the goal of being memorable and standing out from your competition. The goal was to demonstrate something that your brain isn't used to and by extension draw you in just a bit more. Remember, your effort will be recognized and eventually rewarded. Take chances!

Let's get into ego. Not mine, YOURS! Big topic here. Big problems surround your ego. Yeah, mine too. Everyone's.

Feedback is a valuable gift that unfortunately many of us choose to overlook. Personally, I've shied away from seeking feedback from teammates and managers because of my ego. These teammates and supervisors have been in positions many times to observe my sales calls and I've failed myself by not asking for constructive feedback to better myself. I'm guessing you've done the same. Our egos can get bruised easily. We'd simply rather not hear anything other than positive compliments versus critical feedback or constructive critique that may sting a bit. As a result, folks often avoid asking for specific feedback and most certainly avoid asking for areas to improve. Sure, some do, but this is a numbers game, and most don't. The choice to avoid feedback is often based on ego and it's connected to our desire to avoid being told negative things about ourselves. If you could have been close to some of the greatest figures throughout history and witnessed why they fell from power, you'd see that time and time again it was their ego that took them down. It's curious and frustrating why we have an ego in the first place when so much about what our ego does to us impacts us in a negative manner. I get the psychology that we need it to stabilize and protect us when we're lacking confidence, but man, it doesn't seem like an equitable trade off. Regardless, we're hard-wired with an ego, so we should at least know a little about it and how to work with it the best we can.

We all have anxieties and insecurities. Some are more severe than others to be sure, however, there isn't a person among us who doesn't have some emotional fragility, or their own perception of who they are in their mind. When we make a mistake, screw up, or just plain fuck up, and are called out on it, especially in the professional arena, our egos often kick into action. We'll go to the greatest lengths to protect ourselves from admitting wrongdoing, inaction, overreaction, or anything resembling personal responsibility or fault. Our ego, our psychological defense system, doesn't have a built-in mechanism to recognize certain degrees of critique. Our egos jump to the conclusion that we're being attacked, and we respond with an all-or-nothing reaction. We're so quick to protect ourselves from others' observations, beliefs, and critiques that we lose objective reasoning. Our egos are so overly protective, so stubborn, and so lightning quick to protect our sensitivities and insecurities that our realities become unrealities! Put another way, our minds will begin to believe the things that make us most comfortable, even to the extent that they aren't even true!

On the one hand, we're fighting our egos and all the complexities and potentially damaging misperceptions they force us into. While on the other hand, we're dealing with an abundance of leaders that don't have the empathy or interpersonal skills to provide feedback for the sole purpose of improving their teams. Far too many business leaders have no idea how to deliver feedback in the most productive manner. This is a dangerous combination that I'd like to highlight. Attention future leaders, please remember this—You have an ego, quite possibly a stronger one than those you lead. Those you lead have egos and some may have a stronger, more overpowering ego than yours. This is reality. If you don't have tremendous soft skills such as people skills, empathy, and the ability to check your ego while recognizing you're fighting with someone else's ego under your guidance; then you'll fail to break the cycle of a long, distinguished line of bosses that have completely sucked long before you. You want to be a good leader? You want to affect positive change and create a culture where your team doesn't get sick on Sunday afternoons at the thought of coming in on Monday? Learn how to effectively give your team constructive feedback. It's not always entirely possible to choose the most neutral of words in every single circumstance. Too strong of word choice and their egos will most likely destroy the earnest intention you have for growth and improvement for your team. Too soft and you may miss making the exact point needed to be heard, discussed, acknowledged, and agreed upon to move forward. Leaders must understand the fragility of the ego and work with it, not against it. Simply believing or worse, stating, "Don't let your ego get in the way" does nothing but make things worse. It's kinda like the old, "calm down" phrase.

When it comes to feedback or constructive critique, people often take it personally. This, of course, is our ego's ugly head rearing up once again. To take that information personally is a choice, it is usually not the intention of the sender (leader). It's a necessary form of communication to alert someone of what they may have done or are doing incorrectly. It's not easy to provide someone you are leading with constructive criticism and feedback. Some of us know how to deliver and receive feedback more productively and constructively than others. However it's also important for us to accept some personal responsibility. We need to understand and empathize with those in a leadership position that our egos are on high alert, and we should try not attach intent that isn't there. This is where it gets tricky.

Frequently, you'll encounter this ego dilemma. Your boss asks you a question about why you reacted or did something specific, and you immediately become defensive. Maybe you don't go from zero to what the fuck are you saying, but I'm guessing you've seen this or done it before. Our egos interpret the question as if we're being questioned personally, when the other person is asking a question, not questioning us personally. One time, I had a probation supervisor during a debrief question why I reacted in the manner I had reported. My incident report laid out each step I took to break up a serious fight between two rival gang members in the maximum-security unit at San Diego's Juvenile Hall. I immediately became defensive and felt as though I was being interrogated. My supervisor quickly noticed I was tensing up, becoming agitated, and defensive. He paused, lowered his tone, and said, "Sully, I'm not questioning you; I'm asking you a question and I want you to recognize there's a difference." He followed up by telling me that he was asking questions to ensure that his understanding of the report was accurate. He wasn't questioning why I did what I did in the sense that I had screwed up.

It is also critical to recognize that our egos can negatively impact our soft skills. They can negate our soft skills if we're not keeping them under control. Imagine working on improving your soft skills daily and in an instant, your ego flares up, goes into hyperactive mode and BOOM—everything goes to shit! Your ability to effectively communicate is one of the first things to get tossed overboard. The ego, to protect us, sends us a signal that we're being verbally attacked on a personal level, when in most instances, this isn't true. Too late, we're headed up the thermometer to bright red and tunnel vision and selective hearing takes over. Some of us try to hit the brakes as we're noticing it's getting uncomfortable, but our "feedbacker" or "constructive critique listener" isn't too skilled and he or she keeps hitting the wrong button, failing to display any emotional intelligence. Once we hit the red zone, it's all but assured that our communication, empathy, and willingness to consider opposing information is non-existent. We know how these meetings typically end. One or both parties aren't fulfilled, at least, and livid, at worst. The rock is now rolling down negative mountain with zero constructive takeaways. Without having good soft skills and the ability to reassess what occurred and take another shot at the conversation, the relationship can't stabilize and become better.

People with overactive egos fail to give serious focus to others' opinions and ideas. They feel as if their opinion or "way" is the best strategy and suggestions are often met with aggressive rejection. Excessive ego managers or co-workers tend to dominate conversations and don't reciprocate with the same level of active listening. Trying to provide any type of feedback or constructive critique only brings tension, and at times, confrontation. Some people who are less aggressive will silently retaliate once offended as you've bruised their ego and they're not letting it go anytime soon. You may have dealt with these types before or currently have them on your team.

When it comes to teamwork or being a valued member of the team, those with bloated egos arrogantly believe they're the only ones who can do the job. Still worse, they'll at times fail to communicate or delegate out of fear that they'll have to share the credit with another team member. Sounds ridiculous, doesn't it? When teammates begin to recognize that someone's ego is affecting the team atmosphere, a lack of trust develops very quickly. This person is often referred to as a "cancer" within the team. I've rarely seen a turnaround once a team member gets labeled as having too large an ego or labeled as cancerous.

Empathy can also be torpedoed by an unchecked ego. It certainly makes sense that those with over-inflated egos struggle to put themselves in other people's shoes. This is often displayed as insensitivity and is an ugly behavior to witness. It doesn't take long to spot the leader or teammate that is more interested in being right, winning, or dominating than building a team. They are selfish, narcissistic, ugly.

It's ironic that when we hear the word "ego" we tend to attach a negative connotation to it. It does have a purpose and does do good for us as well. Interestingly, those people who have a balanced and healthy ego have confidence and solid mental health. These are the types that aren't afraid to share or even lose competitions within the team. They can show sincere support and aren't jealous of other successes. They're often the leaders, directly or indirectly, and have an easy time building relationships. Their ego attracts everyone around them in interesting ways. Healthy egos don't immediately feel attacked when given feedback or told something that isn't delivered the smoothest of ways. Sure, they can be stunned or hurt, but they react less dramatically and re-center quicker. They're inclined to empathize and evaluate the other person's intent before finalizing judgment and reaction.

Even a slightly inflated ego can disrupt your ability to develop relationships and destroy your reputation in the workplace. Having an over-inflated ego, or even being perceived as having too big of an ego is a one strike and you're out offense. It's too easy in our workplaces to be negatively labeled and this is one label that can be a promotion block all the way up to a career ender. In most professions there's a team element to your job. Even in many sales jobs where you're independently selling for your commissions, you're still part of a larger sales team that must interact, at the very least, within your office space. I've worked with some massively large egos and even had one fellow salesman in my office, early on in my sales career, state the following during a meeting: "I'm not here to make friends, I'm here to make money." Try repeating this to yourself and envision this statement being delivered loudly and proudly to your teammates as you look around the room. This wasn't said under his breath or flippant. He had the floor and made every effort through body language, vocal tone and specifically chosen words to send his message. Our office at this time had a sales manager and there were three of us selling externally and three inside salespeople. I had been on the job for just under a year, and to this day, I have never witnessed nor heard anyone say something so arrogant, so matter of fact and cold, so unconcerned with consequences or perceptions to his character.

Not surprisingly, I worked with this individual for several years and watched him ascend to a sales leadership role. He departed our office and went to manage the next territory north. Ultimately, most of his sales office turned on him and quit. During exit interviews he was verbally torched by those quitting. In fairness, oftentimes those leaving a job can be overly personal and aren't usually the perfect employee. However, there was a consistent and common denominator of feedback from those who he managed. His ego was so incredibly inflated that his arrogance was intolerable. As fate would have it, he ended up fighting with upper management and ultimately resigned under very stressful circumstances.

I wanted to share this story as he was tremendously intelligent, sharp and had most of the skills you could ever want to be a highly successful salesperson (and he was for many years). However, his ego ultimately brought him down from his once pinnacle of tremendous financial success. His reputation, whether deserved or not, is without a doubt forever tarnished by dozens of the professionals he worked for and alongside.

There's a saying I once heard, "One night in Vegas is good, two is great, and three is way too many." Similarly, I've heard a saying about drinking martinis and it's something like, "One martini isn't enough, two is great, and three is too many." These urban myths highlight the delicate balance we must maintain in various aspects of our lives, including the realm of our egos. Our egos are critical and play a pivotal role in shaping our self-perception and, consequently, how we interact with the world around us. They provide us with the needed confidence to navigate life's challenges effectively. However, much like the tempting balancing act of nights spent in Las Vegas or the consumption of delicious martinis, our egos require attentive self-discipline. Be aware and able to surrender to the fact that they often lead us into over-reactive feelings and behaviors that can have lifelong consequences. But above all else, remember this: Never allow yourself to indulge in that third martini on your third night in Vegas, for therein lies a major path to regret.

The ego is the single biggest obstruction to the achievement of anything.

—Richard Rose

Practical Application

May I please propose that you read this list several times?

• **Listen more, talk less with your clients.** Focus on best serving them. Far too often people are trying to impress clients or prospects with what they know or their expertise. This is your ego—check it at the door.

• **Be the first to acknowledge others' accomplishments and celebrate the success of your colleagues.** Often companies will have sales contests, be the one who congratulates the winner first and let them see your sincerity when you high five 'em!

- **Avoid comparisons.** When you're not the sales contest winner, get out of your head immediately and don't let ugly, jealous, ego-centric thoughts creep in like, "I can't believe John won that quarterly sales contest. I'm much better." Keep your focus on you, your own development, and what you can do to get better. Don't allow yourself to feel threatened or jealous of others' achievements.

- **Be honest with yourself about your strengths and weaknesses.** Hold up your mirror consistently and trust what it reveals.

- **Remember the gift of feedback.** Ask your teammates, manager, leader, etc., how you can improve and put the time and effort into doing so. It's there for us every single day, all you gotta do is take a deep breath, open your mouth, and ask for it. Do your best to depersonalize the information and understand it's a challenging habit to master. Routinely asking your team and everyone around you for perspective and insight into what or how you're doing and what could be improved. On this note, don't hesitate to ask what they see you doing well either!

- **Stay humble.** You're not the best salesperson in the world, maybe not even within your own team. Sales is a service profession and your customers' needs should come first.

- **Show gratitude.** Never hesitate to thank teammates or clients who've helped you along the way. Have you ever heard someone say something nice about what you did for them, or recalled something you said even years back, that they've never forgotten? Sometimes it sounds like this, "Ya know a few years back, when you (said/did/gave/etc.), I thought that was impressive and kind of you. I just wanted to make sure, you knew that." There are many versions of this, of course, but it's always a feel-good moment. Let people know when you're grateful, thankful, and appreciative. No matter how hard you've worked, you've never and will never get there alone. Never.

- **It's ok to fail.** True. It really is. We beat ourselves up over it and hold it near and dear far too long. The bigger the failure, the better chance you have of never repeating the steps you took to get there the first time. Learn from failure. Debrief your sales that don't go as you wanted and prepared for. Get some feedback from those who were involved, if any, or talk about what you did with those who have a perspective that will be beneficial.

• **Embrace conflict.** You're not getting out of this profession without facing many of them. The sales profession is explosive in many ways. Your livelihood is being predicated on your ability to connect with someone (yeah, that's the deal gang) and having to unfortunately play a game of chess, while building a relationship. Truthfully, the cost of doing business often will require significant time spent and lost, without reward. The bigger the prize, the harder the competition. So, when the conflicts and the fuck yous start (metaphorically and literally), remember, the loudest nor the most forceful person doesn't win. Know when to say when and walk away, decompress, and re-engage as soon as you're in a place of calm. Nothing positive gets accomplished when two or more people are heated and ratcheting up the negative energy.

Most importantly:

Learn how to say quickly and sincerely:

I. AM. SORRY.

It's distressing and maddening how many people I've come across that simply can't say they're sorry. Yep, it's their ego for sure. Even when smoking-gun-wrong, they can't choke out this simple phrase. Don't be one of these people.

10

You've Got Problems!
Problem Solving

**Never let a 1-day problem
become a 2-day problem.**
—Greg Ellis

Several years back, a dear friend of mine was leaving a career in law enforcement. He had been on patrol, a detective for many years, and ultimately went into a leadership role over a specialty narcotics unit. He had 25 years on the job and one day he asked me what I thought about him coming to work in my company as a salesman. A salesman! Imagine a 25-year veteran police officer thinking they could get into sales! I had a tremendous relationship with this guy, and we had collaborated to run a volunteer charitable organization for about 10 years. I couldn't think more highly of him nor his character. So, when he asked me to setup an interview with my boss, what did I say? Absolutely.

Subsequently, I went in and sat down with my boss before they were scheduled to meet. I told my boss very clearly that there was no way (based on my personal relationship with him), I could deliver less than a "Yes, congratulations! We'd like to hire you." I foolishly was preparing myself for a call from my boss telling me "Greg is a nice person; but I just don't see him in sales." Much to my surprise, my boss called me and said the interview went very well and he was excited to get him started right away. Greg would be working for me, and I would be his sales manager. I was both happy and anxious. What if Greg was a disaster as a salesperson and I was forced to let him go? What if I had to correct him for something he did or said to potentially hurt a deal or flat out lose one? My mind was racing.

Fast forward five years later. Greg turned out to be the best salesman I hired out of eight new hires during my sales management time with that company. To this day, he remains one of the best salespeople I've ever witnessed in a meeting and in the manner with which he develops relationships with his clients. He is that ideal salesperson who has both technical, hard skills and is a master at soft skills. Law enforcement generally doesn't produce individuals with strong interpersonal and soft skills. Those that have them at the beginning regularly lose them during their careers, often due to the daily stress and negative encounters they have with people. The reality is that it can wear down the very best of people regarding their ability to be empathetic and dropping their guard. Empathy and letting your guard down around people generally don't lend themselves to being a successful cop. Law enforcement officers, in general, don't prove to be successful salespeople in positions that require one to reach out to total strangers, develop a relationship, and earn their trust quickly. Greg blew this average right out of the water! And I still stand by it without hesitation. Remember broken watches...he was just that.

Over the course of five years managing Greg, I was constantly impressed by how natural he was dealing with the "fires" that so often occur in packaging distribution. From the first customer crisis he had until the last one I worked through with him, he never failed to approach it calmly and methodically. He had a unique ability to bring his client's level of agitation down quickly. He once stated, "Never let a problem go on to the next day unless you absolutely have to wait for additional information." He went on to say that the faster you tackle a problem head on and hold yourself (and anyone else who made an error) accountable, the quicker your client realizes you're in control of the situation and accepting responsibility.

Greg had an amazing talent for quickly gathering all the relevant information that created or contributed to the problem (this I'm certain was a positive trait from his long-time detective role). Next, he would methodically analyze how the problem evolved and what was done or not done to create it from his side. Then, he'd take a 360-degree approach to everything that could be done to correct the issue immediately or as quickly as possible. Finally, he would get on the phone the moment he had the prior steps under control and deliver the bad news.

Greg would promptly inform his client whenever he realized that he needed additional time to gather information, even if he was aware that the client would face negative consequences. In one situation, I observed him without hesitation tell a client that they were not going to be receiving the prototype they needed for an investor meeting and would miss a critical launch date. I was certain we were going to get serious blow-back, however, the client remained calm and just listened. He was natural at delivering bad news with empathy and his tone and demeanor were always in perfect calm and controlled harmony. He was never afraid to accept responsibility nor apologize if the issue was due to his negligence. Even when it wasn't his fault, Greg never pointed fingers. He knew that clients don't give a damn about your challenges and hurdles, they only want to understand why you screwed up, how fast you're going to correct it, what you will do to make them whole, and what will be done to ensure the same mistake won't happen again. Understandably, not always in that order.

Always be accountable to yourself and your client. My college roommate and dear friend, Chris, gave me several projects throughout my career. Many years back, on an early project, I had screwed up, and he wasn't going to be receiving his boxes that were needed for a trade show. We exchanged emails and I outlined the issue and correction. So, when I saw Chris calling me on the phone, I simply let it go to voicemail as I wasn't ready for the direct ass chewing that I knew was coming. Chris left a voice message that simply said,

"Sometimes ya gotta take the hard calls." I never forgot that day, that message, or its meaning. What a succinct way to say it. It was more of a blow to me because he was (is) such a dear friend. I was taking advantage based on our decades of friendship by avoiding his call at that moment, without really thinking about my responsibility to him as a customer, let alone a friend. I've since added to his statement by stretching it to read as follows: sometimes you gotta take or make, the hard calls.

Mr. Corleone is a man who insists on hearing bad news immediately.
—The Godfather

Bad news, or updated news, which will not be welcome with favor, should be delivered as soon as possible with very little exception. Why deliver bad news the second you're certain there's no getting around it? Time. Time to react and strategize what options exist and in what order to act. For those who have been in sales for many years, we know all too well that a 24-hour delay in bad news can often have a potentially more severe and amplified impact on the client's production schedule or launch date. A day we wait in communicating could be a week or more impact on the client's calendar and needs. I've seen and continue to see numerous professional businesspeople wait and use that old line, "Let's just wait and see what happens." Translation, we don't know what may happen, but something might happen, and we don't have to look vulnerable or apologize. We can pretend it never happened and not risk losing face or hurting our reputation. Of course, there are times where this is a good tactic, but it's a default strategy far too often at the expense of time.

Be proactive in your approach to problem solving when there's a mistake by anyone involved in your business. Don't wait and hope it blows over, don't pretend it didn't happen and never be afraid to apologize when it's required. Get ahead of any problems, especially those that will impact the quality or deliverables of a client's product. Most customers will respect and appreciate the way you step up to inform and advise them of your plan of correction. You might think this is common sense and you'd be incorrect. In my life, across all aspects personally and professionally, shockingly few people I've come across could apologize sincerely and quickly when it was necessary and needed. I can only attribute this to the fragility of our egos or some culturally ingrained, systemic socialization from generation to generation that saying we're sorry equates to weakness.

One year, the largest vendor I used for my business (who was also a large vendor to numerous other salespeople within our company) epically screwed up a teammate's project. My co-workers and manager at the time knew I had the best personal relationship with this vendor and asked me to join them as a show of unity and ensure that we sent a message of total disappointment. This vendor was a family-owned international company. They drove almost three hours to our office and sat in our conference room with eight (seriously pissed off) salespeople and our manager. My manager ran the meeting and walked through the grievance and checklist of issues. When he was finished, both gentlemen representing the vendor began to apologize for their mistakes and ask for both forgiveness and a chance to earn our trust once again.

As I sat and observed our vendors body language and attitude while apologizing, suddenly, a thought came to me. I looked at both gentlemen and I said, "Fellas, we're grateful for your apologies and that you took the time to come down here in person. However, apologies cost nothing. They can be quick, easy, and insincere. When you leave here, how can we know that you aren't laughing on the drive home about how you dodged a bullet or smooth talked your way back into a second chance? I'm not suggesting this is how you feel or what you would do. What I am saying is that apologies cost nothing. You haven't lost the client if we continue to buy from you, although we've lost our customer because of your actions. Worse, who knows what they'll say out in the marketplace? It would be much more meaningful for you to recognize the measurable and significant business loss that we took as a direct result of your mistake. Moreover, offer to split the cost at the very least or credit us back 100% of the loss at best. In addition, we're having our annual holiday party where we ask our primary vendors to contribute to the event. I suggest you guys maximize your contribution over what you've given us in the past, as a show of additional sincerity and generosity to our situation." You could have heard a pin drop, and I thought my manager was going to bust. He was so impressed and energized by my matter of fact, yet respectful, delivery.

The result of my response and request was that we got 50% of our loss refunded and triple what they contributed two years past to our holiday party. The point is that when you make a mistake or your customer suffers for any reason while under your project management, offer something MORE than an apology and a new timeline. Your manager may not like it nor agree with your suggestion, however if the client and their business is important, then why not creatively think of something more than an apology, which costs nothing. It doesn't have to be monumental, but a show of empathy and consideration for your customer that is more than a statement that costs zero dollars. Simply put, have some skin in the apology game.

The ability to problem solve is essential. The ability to display a quick, calm, and confident approach will separate you from your competitors. Because if there is anything, every single salesperson who has held the job for more than a year knows it's this: every single person and company makes mistakes. Regardless of whether you're dealing with a client or negotiating a new or reoccurring contract, the ability to handle problems quickly and effectively will make a huge difference to your sales success. It's also an attractive personal and professional quality that will be well respected by those you serve.

Practical Application

• **Gather all relevant information.** Do this immediately or as soon as the customer has the totality of the problem reviewed. This is a critical first step. Ask for photos or videos if you can, request everything you believe you'll need to understand the entire problem. It's important to keep in mind that you're not interrogating your customer to determine if it was in fact their fault and not yours or your company's. Careful here, if you ask a list of too many robotic questions while your client's hair is on fire, they'll most likely not respond well. This is the time to ask questions, not question your client.

• **Remain calm while displaying a sense of urgency.** Remember that once a problem has come to your attention the client isn't in the happiest or calmest of places. For this reason, your calm and controlled manner are going to serve the entire situation well. Caution here... it's essential to use a calm tone while addressing the client and simultaneously convey a sense of urgency. Work on and practice these types of meetings, calls, e-mails, etc. Stay calm and confident in your tone and demeanor, while ensuring your customer that there is and will continue to be a sense of urgency while correcting the problem.

• **Act quick, but not too quick.** It's critical to analyze the issue and get to your client as soon as possible, however, I've made the mistake of over-reacting and delivering bad news too soon. This does absolutely nothing but aggravate the problem you're trying to solve!

• **Brainstorm.** Get anyone involved that can help you see the situation from outside the fire you are in the middle of. Be creative and open to anything and don't be afraid to try something new. Sound familiar? Getting input from others (teammates, managers, etc.) as they can help you identify blind spots or may have had similar experiences with tried and successful solutions. They may have just the right amount of water for your specific fire.

• **Analyze the risks and benefits of the solutions you're brainstorming.** Consider the potential risks, benefits, and any other message you may or may not be sending with your corrective action. Ideally, you want to select the solution to the problem that has the least risk, but the greatest benefit to your client. Talk through the pros and cons so that when you reveal your solution to the customer, you're less likely to be questioned on how and why you came up with your decision.

• **Debrief.** Review every crisis, every fire drill, and every mistake that was caused by an otherwise controllable error. It's pathetically cliché to write that you need to learn from your mistakes, but there's just no other way to put it. Talk about what and why something happened and what you did successfully, or unsuccessfully, to correct it.

• **Try something new.** Here comes yet another "try something" suggestion. Don't be afraid to take a chance on a new approach even if it doesn't work out. You'll be helping your future self during problem solving. These experiences will provide you with insight in which you can continually revisit. When these professional fires/crisis situations pop up, you'll rely on all your experiences to get you through.

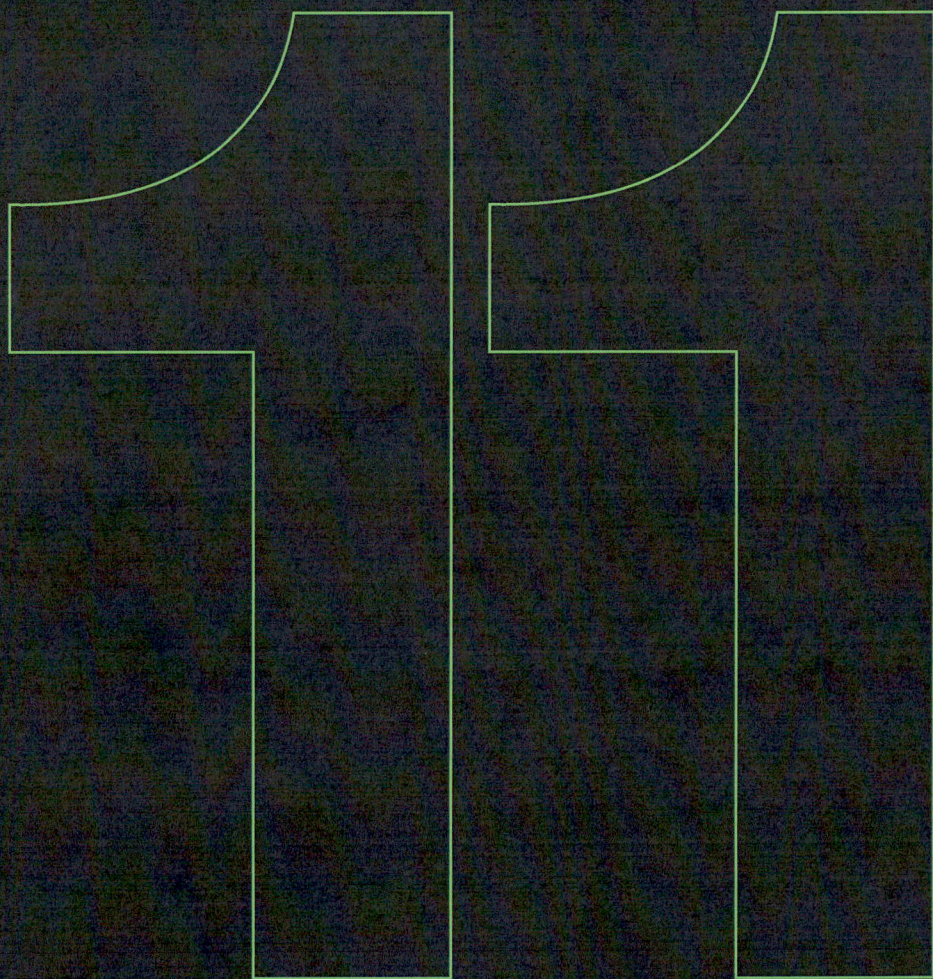

Service Customer Service

You only get one chance to make
a 1st impression and yours may be
in the hands of the receptionist.
—Harvey Mackay

Customer service can be understood as both a noun and a verb, but I'd like to emphasize the aspect of serving clients. There's a wealth of information available on customer service, including best practices and techniques for handling confrontations. However, I want to narrow my focus to the art and skill of being customer centric. This is primarily about who and how we should prioritize our customers. The entire organization should have a unified goal placing the customer at their core. Although salespeople are the primary inter-actors with most customers, there are many people within most businesses that have interactions with and can assist and contribute to the best customer service. It doesn't matter your title or role, if you're in business, you're servicing your customers. Everyone you touch and interact with can have a positive or negative impact on your business. Strive to treat everyone that comes in your contact with kindness, and you'll never have to cross a burned bridge.

One afternoon in Riverside, CA, I was with Greg (my law enforcement turned salesman friend). We were making classic walk in the lobby cold calls. Not to ask to talk to anyone, but simply to try and get a business card to add to our target lists. But hey, ya never know, there have been times that walking in the lobby got me a meeting right then and there (you know those dumb luck broken watches ☺). I'll never forget this specific call because it was a security and personal protection distributor/manufacturer (think police gear). Remember, Greg is a 25-year police veteran, and I am a medically retired police officer, so I've got my retirement badge ready to "flash" to try an old routine that I've used dozens of times before. Visualize me walking towards the receptionist and as I approach, I produce my retirement badge and announce that I'm a local (insert city) detective and need to speak with so and so. Not sure how it lands when you read it but let me assure you that it killed 95% of the time that I used it. It was always good fun and seconds after the startled looks on faces that had no idea what to do, I'd smile and admit I was playing a practical joke and was there for a sales call. I often followed up saying I was retired, which always lead to some good conversations. Use what ya got! Props work amazingly well, as do great stories.

I'm walking in thinking we have the perfect background to connect with whoever is behind the desk. We open the door and walk into a very nice, large, professional lobby. We noticed there's no receptionist as we got to the front desk and of course we were very disappointed. Just as we turn to head out, we hear a voice saying, "Can I help you guys?" Great! We both think we're going to get a chance to connect with someone.

The man proceeds to tell us he's the VP of Operations (how lucky we were!) and then begins telling us in an oddly aggressive manner that he has no need for whatever we're selling nor the time to talk to us. We hadn't even gotten out why we were there (which was simply to grab a business card of the person who purchased their packaging so we could CALL BACK another day and schedule an appointment). The guy kept on and suddenly, Greg stopped him right in his tracks. I'll never forget it as this was the first time I've seen or heard what came next.

Greg says, "Excuse me. Why the attitude? Why are you coming at us so aggressively? You guys sell protective police equipment here, yes?" The man replied, "Yeah, we do." Greg then went on to say, "You must then have a sales department, yes?" The guy replied, "We do." Greg replied, "Good then understand that we sell packaging and we're in sales. You sell protective gear and have a sales team that does exactly what we're trying to do. Would you ever want them treated by a potential client like you're treating us right now? All you had to do was be kind and let us introduce ourselves and why we're here, and then tell us how happy you are with your current supplier(s), and we would have thanked you for your time and been on our way. That simple. I just don't understand why you had to be so unkind about us stopping in. Everyone is trying to sell something." The guy appeared a bit stunned and had nowhere to go with a reply.

At this moment Greg turned around and we headed towards the door. Greg, who was noticeably agitated, stopped, and turned around one last time. He said, "Think about how we walk out this door and go off into our jobs wherever they take us. You had a chance to be an ambassador for your company and you've done the opposite." Out the doors we went, and I was knocked out. I'd never seen such a reply or interaction. I'd been on hundreds of walk-in-the-building cold calls with numerous other reps. I'd been responded to and reacted to negatively hundreds of times simply due to walking in a lobby for a contact name. I'd never seen an interaction like this. Greg was 100% right on. Non-negotiable, no apologies, just hit the guy between the eyes just as he deserved. Now, were we ever going to get a chance to do business there? Unlikely. We knew it, but what we knew more was that it felt good to swing back just once on a rude person who was disrespectful and unnecessarily aggressive.

My take-away was the pure genius of what Greg had just said to the prick. Most of us are selling something, at some time, to someone. We're all selling. Why not recognize the challenges of selling during those times you're "the buyer" and respectfully, pleasantly, and empathetically tell the salesperson, "No thank you. We're quite happy with who we have for your X or Y." Now, if you're trained by your sales manager to attempt to overcome that objection and keep pushing with all the old school tricks and phrases that are sup- posed to change their mind, I can't help you here. You've now just invited the potential for frustration and agitation. No matter how smooth you are, you blew the professional and social cue to politely leave. Sure, you could walk out with a purchase order or sale, but I highly doubt it.

It's disheartening to see such a significant decline in the "put the customer first" service mentality. The reputation that the U.S. once held for exceptional customer service is quickly fading away and becoming nothing more than a nostalgic memory of better days. Because of this rapid decay, we should change the order of the words when we say customer service. We've grown complacent around the absolute importance of this phrase and its title in the workplace. A friend of mine recently was talking about the utter lack of customer service and he said, "It's the new world we live in, customer service just sucks."

Even worse still and my biggest pet peeve are the companies that outsource their "customer service" to foreign countries. These poor people are getting paid a fraction of an American wage and having to read from scripts that give standard, and quite often, less than helpful resolutions. Not only do these companies save a large percentage of money, but they further benefit from what I call the "wear down" effect. Most of us simply give up and stop pursuing action on our complaints.

CUSTOMER SERVICE

Perhaps if we began saying "service customer" instead of "customer service," we would hear and repeat the action, and reset the emphasis and priority on our customers. Please understand that all salespeople wear many hats, and one of those hats is in customer service. This isn't a section to address only those who are specifically assigned to customer service or inside sales. While it will serve those well, it's intended to bring you, salespeople, back into the mindset that you are, in fact, a customer service representative, in addition to being a salesperson for your customers.

There is one sentence that you should rehearse, role play and entirely memorize when it comes to handling an upset customer. Ready? Here it goes, and it's my hope you'll read it several times and let it really sink in.

What can I do to make this right for you, right now?

Of course, this would be preceded with an apology (if necessary or required) or at the very least an expression of empathy so that you display an understanding of how your client is feeling. Depending on what the industry and issue is, there is a good chance that you won't be able to do anything immediately to help solve the problem. That's irrelevant for the purposes of the statement. Asking what you can do right now is the most soothing phrase an upset customer can hear. This is meant to de-escalate a client or person in a heightened emotional state because of something you are responsible for, either directly or perceived. Practice it and truly embrace it. The more sincere you can make the statement, the stronger it becomes at bringing someone who is angry down to a place where they are less likely to attack and risk making communication worse, both ways. Ideally, you can and will quickly pursue the answer or action necessary to make the customer whole. In the event you can't, using this sentence will allow the conversation to be much more productive and less aggressive.

No news is bad news.

Don't forget that if you commit to a timeline or specific "will reply by time/date," you can't blow it. If you drop the ball or your company does and you're the CSR or sales rep, you better update on your committed time and date whether you have anything or not. Silence is not your friend here. This old habit is prevalent and so foolish! "I'm sorry, I hadn't heard from my…our…the… so I was waiting to contact you Mr./Mrs. customer…" Abso-fucking-lutley never do this. Never! Never! Never!

If you can't put yourself in the mindset of the customer as to why this is so senseless, lazy, and borderline unprofessional, being in sales or service may not be for you. Mistakes happen, people screw up, and products are damaged, every single day, in every single industry. Everyone knows this, but what they need to know is that you understand why they're upset, ask them what you can do to make them better right now, and provide them with a firm, specific will reply-by date if needed. It's that simple.

We won't win or be perfect in every deal, but we can win every response time!

When you think of customer service positions, one of the first that comes to mind is probably the receptionist. It's unfortunate that so many new salespeople will likely never have the experience of engaging with a fantastic receptionist. One of the most under-appreciated and undervalued customer service positions, most certainly is the receptionist. The receptionist is the very first person you meet upon entering a company's front door. This is a company's face, voice, personality, and ambassador. The receptionist, or (R), as I would regularly note in my planner when cold calling and keeping notes for later calls, is also the last face and person you see from a company when leaving the building. This person is your first and last impression to the outside world of visitors, as well as your internal world for all those employees coming in and leaving through the front. Think about that. These individuals could brighten your day with a simple smile or even better, detect your mood simply by seeing you every day and becoming familiar with your body language. To all the receptionists who ever lived and held this position, my hat is off to the good ones. Because they weren't all great. Just like everything else, there were goods ones and bad ones.

I tried to calculate how many buildings, companies, and by extension, receptionists I've encountered over my 20+ years of selling and I'm conservatively putting this number around 1,250 receptionists. The best I ever dealt with was a woman named Pat. I'll never forget her. Early in my career, I was given a rare somewhat "warm" lead to an up-and-coming medical device company in San Diego. I was still very green, so I was a bit anxious and nervous upon my arrival (20 minutes early). Upon checking in, I smiled and said hello. The usual formalities and pleasantries began, and Pat asked who I was there to see. I told her and she began asking questions about my company and what we did and who I was, in the sincere "tell me about you" manner that is missing in so many initial conversations. I finally said, "Pat, I'm nervous. I gotta tell ya, I really want to make a good impression and nail this first meeting. I just wanted to say that your kindness, warmth, and willingness to chat with me has been remarkably kind. Thank you." She replied, "Jason, you're going to do great, and Tom (the buyer) will love you. Don't worry about a thing. Be yourself and if you feel like you're not making headway, bring up the University of Michigan as Tom went there. You'll be set." She winked and smiled. I smiled back. Tom came out and brought me into his office moments later. For 10 years, three company site moves and numerous staff changes and promotions I held on to most of the packaging for this account and gained some lifelong friends. Friends that I'm still in contact with via social media and in person 10+ years later and 1800 miles away, Pat (R) included. ☺

Customer service is eroding rapidly in our country. The "Pats" are fewer and farther between. So much so that's it unnerving to those from older generations who experienced what once was the standard level of service. The most disturbing fact of the decline in customer service is the outsourcing of it. If any company truly, honestly held the belief that their customers were the most important component of their business, they would never, and could never, outsource this service. It's obvious that most large businesses who outsource their customer service numbers don't truly believe in taking care of their clients. It's incomprehensible that a company would put the responsibility of fielding customer complaints, troubleshooting, or any less than positive issues to foreign countries simply to save money. I've lived abroad and taught English to residents of other countries. Learning English as a second language is challenging and even more difficult to utilize when dealing with an upset American regarding bad product or services. So, why in the world would you ever take a person from a foreign country, who doesn't speak fluent English to handle your customer service calls? For those individuals that can speak fluent English, the vast majority, have such a heavy accent that you're forced to pay twice as much attention to make sure you're understanding what they're saying. It doesn't stop there because the connection is 500 million miles away and sounds every bit of it. The one that pushes me right off the edge is the dissonance of background conversations – the other 2,334 customer service reps fielding calls simultaneously. Topping off the frustration by the effort needed to decipher heavy accents and a strained connection, all your energy is devoted to grasping the next steps or what they can't or won't do!

What could possibly make someone upset? The entire reason customer service is a department, is a skill, is a thing, is to help assist the people who buy your stuff and receive their stuff the way it was marketed, sold, and promised. Mistakes happen, but why would you drop the ball and put the team and department that is meant to calm and correct situations, in the hands of people that can't communicate fluently and efficiently with your customers? Honestly, nothing says "I don't give a fuck about my customers" quite like foreign outsourcing the one department that is solely intended to service your customers! It's dejecting, enraging and simply insane what we're forced to go through to struggle to understand, just to be told no! This lack of engagement and empathy represents the height of arrogance and selfishness in current business practices. I highlight my feelings with the intention to ensure you DO NOT EVER fail your clients with customer service. Always service your clients and they'll stay with you longer than you ever thought imaginable.

Remember back when I explained the historical failure of telling someone to "calm down" and how it just doesn't work. Well, I recently had a customer service agent tell me to "Please watch my mouth." You know what happened next? I said, "Yes, you're right, I'm so very sorry for being upset and I don't mean to use bad language. What else may I adjust about my attitude right at this moment when I've waited 11 minutes on a phone tree to hardly hear you and now be told you don't appreciate my attitude?" I most certainly did not respond this way. I snapped and gave this poor service rep both barrels. I did, however, have the ability before I went nuts to explain it wasn't a personal attack on him, but rather a reflection of his company (and I hoped he was recording). Ok, I may be a bit triggered by this, but I can promise you that in general, using that phrase as a customer service professional (or as a supervisor in customer service) does nothing to calm down an agitated and upset client. Rather, it's equivalent to throwing gasoline on a fire. Why anyone in customer service would use this phrase is beyond me. First, if a customer is using profanity and noticeably upset, the last thing you want to do is tell them to "watch their mouth." There's a clear difference between, "You fucking idiot! Why would you send the wrong product to me?" and "What the hell is wrong with the shipping department?" Verbally assaulting a person versus the company, are clear, distinct, and separate verbal outbursts. Rarely does a person attack a specific individual without cause in the early phases of engaging with customer service reps. It's generally after they've acted in the wrong way that an already agitated, upset customer reacts to an unskilled customer service rep.

In an ideal world, nothing goes wrong when we pay for a product or service. Everything is perfect and our money is well, sometimes even, very well spent. But every now and again things go wrong. Sometimes, they're small issues and other times they're large issues. Who do we turn to? Our sales rep or the company's customer service department. Their job is to correct the problem and return the customer to a satisfied state. How many times has this not happened to you? If you're going to take on the role of a professional salesperson, or customer service representative, please understand that it's now your responsibility to un-fuck anything and everything that comes your way. There's no passing the buck in customer service. You're the salesperson who is earning a salary or the commission from the sale. It's your baby and yours alone.

Here are a few tips to demonstrate outstanding customer service, whether you're a salesperson or the actual customer service representative within your company. Just remember, if you're a salesperson, *you're customer service* as well!

Practical Application

- **Be quick to respond and courteous to customer service needs and requests.**

- **Listen, listen, and listen (actively) some more.** Make certain you're clear on whatever it is that has them upset, disappointed, or unclear.

- **Display empathy.** Acknowledge and validate the customer's feelings. A simple "I can understand why/how you feel this way…" goes a long way.

- **Avoid using the words "no" and "unfortunately."** These instantly increase tension from an already disappointed (at best) to a very upset (at worst) customer. Find alternative ways to get your point across. Instead of "No, we don't have anyone higher than myself available," try rephrasing that to "My boss will be in tomorrow at 2 pm. I could take your information and leave him/her an urgent message, or you are free to call back at that time." Just a simple little twist in your word choice dramatically takes the edge off the knife. Words matter. Really matter.

- **Go above and beyond to ensure that your customer is satisfied.** Do this to every extent possible (as it usually is possible). Follow up with them after the issue has been resolved to demonstrate that you are still concerned about their problem and want to ensure they're now feeling cared for.

• **Take responsibility and be accountable.** Even if the customer's issue has nothing to do with anything you've done or not done, own it. Take the lead and be the person that can and will handle their concerns. Not only is this honorable, but it displays that your professional role is to be their primary point of contact who is responsible for every aspect of the sale (even when the customer may know it wasn't your fault). If anyone gets an ass chewing, you take it.

• **Be proactive.** If you want to avoid being on the wrong end of a dissatisfied client's call, anticipate customer needs and offer proactive solutions before something goes sideways.

• **No news is NOT GOOD NEWS.** When you're responsible for updating a customer on anything they're waiting for, never, ever, never avoid calling them because you have no updates. No update demands an update to your customer that there is no update. Get it? When a customer is waiting and wanting something, simply receiving nothing is maddening. Why? Primarily because their mind is wandering and racing that you've forgotten, you're too busy with other matters or worse still, you have no sense of urgency for their order. Eliminate all of these with a quick phone call, every X number of hours/days, putting their mind slightly at ease that at the very least, that YOU are NOT forgetting about their "stuff."

• **Never ever never use the phrases "calm down" or "watch your mouth" when dealing with an upset customer.** They're rarely irate at you, but at your company's failure. Should you happen to go ahead and let your ego take off and use these lines; I promise you'll escalate the situation and most often give the agitated customer the motivation they need to keep on pushing their complaint up the ladder ■

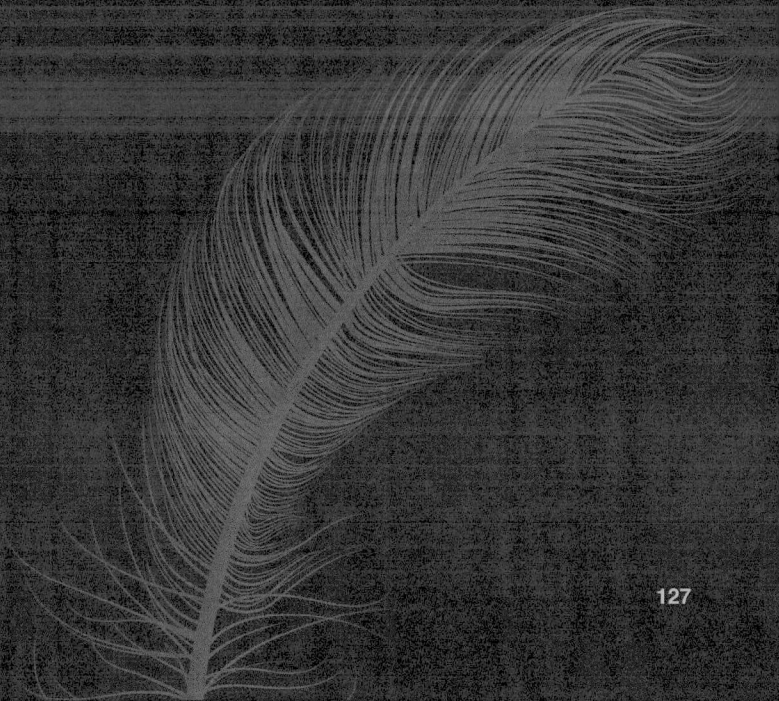

The 100 Pound Telephone

Selling to people who actually want to
hear from you is more effective than
interrupting strangers who don't.
—Seth Godin

When I initially planned this chapter, I intended to title it "-100 Degrees: The Coldest of Cold Calling." However, I came across an old sales term that I found fascinating and felt compelled to share it in case you haven't ever come across it. The term is the "100-pound telephone," which refers to making a cold call or contacting someone for a difficult conversation that needs to take place. As soon as I heard this expression, I promised myself that I wouldn't forget it and I'd use it in any future sales training courses I taught, as well as for this chapter. It captures the essence of the uncomfortable stress and challenges that most people face when making cold or difficult phone calls. If you're unfamiliar with the phrase the "100-pound telephone," I hope it brings a smile to your face and makes ya think, "Yup, that just about describes it," just like it did for me.

I wanted to devote a significant chapter to cold calling. You won't necessarily find "cold calling" on any soft skills lists; however, it absolutely falls under the following related soft skills: communication, listening, empathy, and charisma, to name a few. It's such a major part of most sales responsibilities that I simply had to include a chapter dedicated to this most critical aspect of sales. In full transparency, my initial book was penciled in to be solely on the art of cold calling. Also, in no small part, I happen to have years of experience doing it and still do it well. That doesn't mean I like it (at all), in fact quite the opposite. But I want to share some of my insight and experiences in hopes that others may learn, improve, and benefit.

Cold calling is the absolute worst part of being in sales. Full stop. Very few times in my 22-year career have I ever met a salesperson who has said, "I love cold calling." Let me just make this clear right now. Anyone who says this is full of shit. They're full of shit, they're brand new, or they've had a head injury. Ok, maybe I'm slightly exaggerating. But there's nothing enjoyable about picking up a telephone and dialing a number where you have no idea who is going to be picking up the call; or what type of attitude they'll have (if they pick up the call at all). Furthermore, for you gamblers, the odds that the person who picks up the call will be less than happy and pleasant are as close to perfect as you could ever get. Being on the receiving end of a miserable, unhappy, agitated person who seizes the opportunity to tell you how bothersome and disruptive (be it directly or indirectly) to their day you are gets old and personal, very quickly. Gets personal? Yep, it sure does.

The one thing you should never do when cold calling is interpret the recipient's rude behavior personally. That's what the "manual" says. By "manual" I mean the longstanding belief and teaching of sales leaders across the world since forever. After all, the person who picks up your cold call has no idea who you are, how you are, where you've been and come from, and most importantly, what kind of person you are. All they know is that you've gotten them to pick up the phone, when they didn't want to, and they have no interest in hearing what you have to say. I'm going to come back to personalization later, but for now understand that it takes a special temperament and skill to make daily, numerous cold calls and NOT personalize rude behavior.

It's one thing to cold call a total stranger when you're representing a product or service that is either alone in its space or in minimal company. It's entirely another when you pick up that phone and represent a packaging distributor, which represents one of the top five largest industries in the world. Talk about over-saturated. Packaging salespeople make real estate agents look sparse (I tease real estate agents and have nothing but love for them). I never imagined how awful this most primary responsibility of being a salesperson was until the first week of my first sales job.

My routine was to go out in my car and hit business parks and try to broach the company through the back door warehouse and if that didn't work, drive around the front, and meet the receptionist. I was told to get business cards or contact names for the company and come back and cold call them. Rinse and repeat every day until I had enough business to pause and focus on project management and relationship building.

I've experienced the gamut from when just about every business you walked into had some form of receptionist to companies that eliminated that position and have a bell at the desk or a directory and phone dialing instructions to make contact inside. Nowadays, doors are locked, windows are blacked out, and security cards are required to open the door. Times have changed. I don't want to be "that guy" and talk about the "good ole days," but in this instance, it's necessary to go backward to understand how I can help you going forward.

Knocking on the door to introduce yourself and trying to make a strong impression is essentially gone, at least for those calling on Tier I and II sized businesses. Today we rely on LinkedIn, social media, and a variety of lead generation services to try to get over the wall, or around the gatekeeper. However, anyway you approach it, sooner or later you'll need to make your first call. This is still a cold(er) call in that you have never spoken to this individual in your life. Whether you are dialing a number for the first time, going in personally to meet someone, or you are virtually meeting people; they all have one thing in common, it's your very first time. Usually, it's "cold" that very first meeting. You're not sure what type of person you'll be communicating with, which makes your soft skills that much more critical. The ability to adapt and flex to the behavior style of your new target never goes unused.

Understand this before you spend another day in your sales career or take a step forward to becoming a salesperson. The entirety of your salesmanship and ability to be your best will be more successful if you believe in the good or service you are selling. By believe, I mean really believe in its worth and value to others. It's an even stronger force when you understand what unique value your company brings to their industry. What do you do or have that's different from your competitors?

If you give a damn about your product or service, it will come through over the telephone, in person, and in your writing (text, e-mails, etc.). If you wouldn't buy, use, or personally stick your neck out for the good or service you are selling, I've got news for you, you'll lead a mediocre and unfulfilling sales role, at best, or ultimately fail, at worst. Unless you've got a nice blend of narcissism, sociopathic ambition, and the worst commission breath of all time, you'll eventually hate what you do.

Let me tell you about my first big league cold call. Remember I mentioned how I began my sales career halfheartedly? Go back there for a moment with me as I tell this story. At that time, half-assing was still my daily attitude and pace. One day at the local gym, simply being my social self, I was provided with the opportunity to meet a gentleman named Mike. I'd seen Mike many early mornings arriving at the gym at the same time as I did. Eventually, we began talking and in no time, we developed a friendship. Not an atypical story by any means. Mike was a few years older than I but had the charisma and energy that I had always hoped I had and surely wanted to be like. Yes, I wanted to be like Mike. Beal and Jordan, too!

My San Diego office was near the golf capital of the world, yet no one in my company had been able to break into that industry. Over the weeks to come, Mike and I would chat about what he did; turns out he was VP of sales for a golf shaft company. Mike asked what I did. I replied, "I sell packaging." That simple reply would be the springboard for the conversation that would ultimately lead me to a successful career in packaging sales. Mike replied, "Packaging, as in boxes?" I replied, "As in everything packaging: boxes, foam, poly bags, labels, print, marketing collateral, you name it."

Mike (who remains a close friend to this day) proceeded to tell me that he would happily introduce me to a woman he knew well in Callaway Golf, and he thought she may be in packaging purchasing. Of course, I immediately jumped at his offer, got her number, and called her (that very same morning). She was beyond friendly and so easy to speak with that I felt like I just got a win!

Unfortunately, she was not the person that I needed to speak with. She gave me the name and number of the gentleman I needed to call. Damn it! Another degree of separation. So close…The man that I needed to speak with was Darren Davis and I was given his direct line. He was a packaging buyer for Callaway Golf at the time. I recall being a bit nervous prior to the call as this would be the largest company, I had cold called up to this point in my almost two years of cold calling.

Butterflies swirling in my gut, I pick up the phone, begin dialing and it starts ringing…"Hello, this is Darren." The tone of Darren's voice was that of a grizzly bear. It was rough, serious, and carried a deep projection. Not the type of voice you want to hear when already anxious to engage in a cold call sales pitch. In fact, intimidating voices on a scale of one to Clint Eastwood, I'd have to say that Darren's voice was the most menacing phone voice I've ever heard (and still is to this day). All I could think at that second was, I'm in it now and there's no way I'm getting this bear to relax and give me a chance. I started with the very generic introduction, "Hi Darren, my name's Jason Sullivan. I'm calling to see if we could connect and talk about your current packaging." Pause, five, four, three, two, one. It was at this moment that somehow, someway, I managed to toss out the script that I'd written out on a notepad and spit out something I'd never stated, nor consciously thought before. This impromptu change would go on to transform my sales career.

The phone call went like this. "Hold on, Darren, the truth is, we both know that if I quote your packaging, I'll be within 5-10% of what you're currently spending based on my knowledge of who is currently providing your packaging. I could be slightly more, ideally slightly less. However, that doesn't matter. Because if you don't like me, I may not get past this call and on to the true opportunities that would benefit both Callaway and me. Would you be willing to meet for a beer after work one evening on your way home? My treat and I promise at the very least, it'll be a cold beer and we'll have some laughs. If I can't separate myself from the competition in 30 minutes based on my personality, attitude, and energy, then at least we tried. I know my company is large enough to support anything you have on your desk and I'm certain you know this. However, what you don't know is what kind of guy I am. Am I trustworthy? Any fun to work with? Communicative, proactive, and overall, someone you wouldn't hesitate to pick up the phone to call? The kind of sales rep you wouldn't run away from if they were trying to reach out to speak with you. You know the type, the ones you dread having to call?"

Darren laughed and then paused. His three second pause felt like an hour in real time (due to my anxiety and eagerness). My mind in those few seconds was racing. What did I just say? Where did it come from? How did it roll off my tongue so naturally? Most pressing, how in the hell was he going to respond? Seconds later Darren growled, "Yeah, I can do that." That was it. No acknowledgment of my on the spot go for it words that took me by total surprise. We scheduled a beer on that Friday after work and the rest is history. Callaway Golf was my first six figure purchase order and I went on to be one of their top packaging suppliers for the better part of 15 years.

Darren left a few years after getting me in the door. Over the years Darren and I became good friends, and I was fortunate enough to get to know his beautiful family. One day, I received a call from his wife (his childhood sweetheart) that Darren had a heart attack and passed away. He was in his mid-40's at the time of his death and it was, as you can imagine, very upsetting. Darren, if you're reading this up in heaven, please know that I've never forgotten that first phone call, that first beer, nor all your kindness and guidance during my early years. Your willingness to give a new guy a chance made all the difference to my career and my life. Your kindness set off a professional confidence within me that allowed me to engage and assert myself to another level. See you again one day my dear friend, the cold beers, of course, will forever be on me.

Before you start to dial your cold calls, it's best to manage your expectations. There's an age old saying in sales that goes something like this, it takes 100 calls to get 10 appointments to get one sale. I've heard this ratio twisted slightly in a few different ways; however, the point is you're going to experience a significant amount of rejection before you're rewarded with a sale. I think I heard something before that a career batting average of .290 gets a pro baseball player into the Hall of Fame. That's a surprisingly low percentage on its face. It speaks of the difficulty of the game, of course, as does the 100:10:1 sales ratio to the degree of difficulty of cold calls. The curse and the beauty of cold calls in sales is that on one hand you're going to make dozens of calls before you get someone to engage and listen to you, yet on the other, it takes just one call to make your day, week, month, quarter and sometimes year! One call! It's impossible for you to know the moment the phone rings, whether there's an opportunity on the other end of the line. You've got to make the call to get the opportunity to discover if it can be great. It all starts with dialing a number.

This one potential "yes" is what keeps salespeople going. The "what if" home run scenario on the other end of the line from a list of hundreds of potential targets. That feeling when timing meets preparation. Yep, so much of sales is plain ol' dumb luck. You read that right. But don't think for a moment there isn't a method to improve that dumb luck. It's the part most of us don't like. To increase your odds of luck working in your favor, you need to increase your number of calls, visits, e-mails, messages, attempts, and efforts to give lady luck the best chance at stopping on your number. Cold calling is challenging and can be painful at times which is why it's so difficult. The will and persistence to keep trying separates the best of salespeople.

**The magic you're looking for is in
the work you're avoiding.**
—Dipen Parmar

The phone is ringing, and someone is about to answer…You should be a little anxious, at least a little bit. Anything important to us should heighten our senses at least a little. What are you going to say when someone picks up your cold call? You have one chance, only one, to instantly grab their attention. This is that moment where you never get a second chance to make a first impression. It's show time!

The creative and unique way in which you deliver the purpose of your call to the receiver separates the good from the average, and bad. For example: "Hi, my name is, I'm calling from…We do…I was hoping to speak with you about…." This is generic and average and the person who uses this tactic was also voted most likely to never get a second date in this example. Safe, scripted, and yawwwwn producing. You might as well start off by saying, "Please let me down easy…."

To craft a short, quick, and to the point attention grabbing pitch, YOU need to spend some time on it. Serious time. Cold calling doesn't require you to be the smoothest, quickest witted, or most intelligent person on the phone. It simply requires that you're not robotic and give the call something different than the usual lines.

Begin with something different and state why you're calling (quickly). After all, think about it, you're a total stranger and the clock is ticking. Get to the damn point quickly. Very quickly. Even before you give your name! "Hi, I wanted to see if we could schedule a meeting next week at your convenience to discuss your current packaging inventory management system. I work for the largest packaging distributor in the U.S. and we're hearing from numerous new clients that they have space and logistics challenges. We fix these problems quickly and in many cases at a neutral price point if we can't save you some money. My name is Jason and I work for X."

Never run on and over your receiver on the call. If they're speaking, you need to shut it down. Be cognizant of their tone, tempo and listen to their vocal cues that should tell you their emotional state. Many times, it's just not the right time to engage someone. You risk being brushed off or worse labeled as irritating and bothersome if you can't read visual, vocal, or verbal cues. Being persistent isn't always the best course. That fine line of being persistent versus being a pain in the ass should be something you acquaint yourself with as soon as possible.

Put yourself in a buyer's shoes right now. You've most likely received a cold call from someone with very little creative effort. What happens the second you recognize they're trying to get you to listen so they can sell you something? You want out of the situation immediately! The moment they say "I know you're busy, I just have one final question…" is the moment you get triggered and that all but ensures it's over. That's just the way it is.

Shorter is sweeter and less is usually more. This may sound easier than it is to do. There's a quote by an unknown author that reads, "If I had more time, I would've written a shorter letter." The attention, focus and energy required to be succinct is often avoided. Most of us would rather write it, say it, or type it the way it comes from our mind the very first time. To pause, evaluate our thought or sentence, and then consciously go back and revise our message with fewer words takes too much time and mental effort.

When preparing to make cold calls, you want to make sure that you can smoothly, quickly, and efficiently make your point. The goal is to let your potential client know WHY you're calling, quickly introduce yourself and company, and then lay out a call to action. This takes 30 seconds on the long side. Consider your cold calls to be identical or very similar to the classic elevator pitch (also 30 seconds or less).

This may be the only time I would advocate for memorization. You want to be able to quickly tell someone what you do and why they may need and want the good or service you're selling without being too wordy or long winded. Remember people's attention spans are embarrassingly short. Memorizing your cold call-elevator pitch isn't a bad thing. What is bad is delivering it as if you just memorized it. Plan on nauseating amounts of rehearsal and repetition so that you can repeat it naturally, adding inflection and emphasis as well as handle any interruption to it without losing your place. Yes, this is the one time memorizing what you should say to a potential customer is highly recommended. I can't think of any other time that memorizing a statement or thought is needed.

Spend the time while you have it, as you never know when you might run in to someone who asks you what you do with the intention of wanting to do business with you. Have your elevator pitch (also cold call pitch) flawlessly locked in and be ready to say it with confidence and style so it's not robotic nor rehearsed to the ear. You'll play as you've practiced. Those instantaneous cold call moments can get really warm if you're prepared and handle them with poise and confidence.

If all goes well and you get an interested person on a cold call from your first effort, ensure you're prepared. Now is the time to ask questions and display that you are problem solving to achieve a goal. Remember, the MOST IMPORTANT QUESTION you can ask is what their pain point or business challenge/needs are right now. If you can uncover these early in a conversation, you now have the keys to their heart. All you need to do is tell them clearly how your product or service can and will fix their specific problem. The more specifically you can explain how you have their fix the better. Discovering a company's immediate needs or challenges before a cold call will pleasantly surprise you with how much warmer the call will be.

I just summarized what I believe is the most efficient way to open the cold door to achieve sales greatness. You have the answer to the test. All the bullshit, fancy terms, tricks, tips, ideas, and methodology that you've ever read, saw on Tik Tok, or Googled boiled down to the same goal. When you DON'T have the business and you want the business, all you need to do is this:

Discover what their pain and needs are right now. Be able to tell them specifically (not generally, not from inferring, implying, or illustrating possibilities) how your medicine alleviates their sickness.

It's not always easy, but it's rarely too difficult to get someone to open up about their needs and stresses that they want fixed.

Most of us know that the return rate on cold calling rarely appears like the best use of time. It's hard to argue with the numbers that if you call 100 people, maybe you get 10 to talk, and one appointment out of it. However, and I'll repeat it again, it's that one call that can change a career. One call has changed numerous salespeople's careers and lives. This is why it's still done in many industries. As new ways of communicating evolve, the old-fashioned cold call will still be with us for quite a while to come.

To leave or not to leave a message, that is the question! Generally, we're going to get someone's voicemail when cold calling.   They see our number and automatically believe it's spam if it's unrecognizable. I'm a believer in leaving voice messages most of the time. Certainly, the first time you get a voicemail, but even on a regular cadence as you're remaining persistent. Maybe don't leave one every week when following up (although I often did.) If you're going to be like everyone else and leave a generic, standard message, absolutely don't do it. You'll be tuned out quickly. However, if you mix it up, be creative, and personalize, you'll greatly increase the chance for a call back or future pick up.

When I was just starting out cold calling in the very earliest and purest days of my career, I would keep a written log of who and when I called someone. I would note if I left a voicemail or not. My cadence at the time was no more than one call per week (mixing up the day and time).

One day, on week 16 calling a particular target, this is what happened. In case you missed that, I just wrote week 16th. I had cold called and left a message for a particular target every single week for sixteen weeks. On this day, the prospect's voicemail picked up and I started in a slightly different manner. Truth be told, I was running out of creative ways to leave messages, as well as gas. I said, "Hi Nick, it's Jason Sullivan calling for the 16th week in a row. I know it's the 16th week because I'm staring at a notepad that shows each time, I've left a voice message and I just tallied week 16. I'm sorry to bother you and take up space on your machine once again. However, I've reached that competitive point where I simply can't and won't give up until I've at least gotten five minutes on the…" Suddenly someone picked up the phone and said, "Jason! I can't take it anymore. I had to pick up and talk to ya. I had to put a real time voice with this voice message person I've been hearing for months! Ok, you've got five minutes so let's hear it." Nick was holding back laughs the entire time he was saying this, and I knew at that moment, I'd at least have his attention and possibly an opportunity to meet up.

This is what I call the persistence plan. Understand this is high risk but also very high return, and should be used appropriately, not with every target. Once again, it's important to maintain that fine line between being a pain in someone's ass and professionally persistent. Professionally persistent vs. being obnoxious. How to tell? A good barometer for the success of your cold call is the duration of the call and how many questions were asked by the target. If target clients aren't responding to follow up calls, chances are they weren't interested in what you said or even maybe the way you delivered the information.

I've always found that when a salesperson cold calls me, the moment I tell them I'm not interested if they say anything other than, "I understand and hope you have a wonderful day," I become agitated. There is no chance they can say or do anything to bring me around. Be cognizant and pick up on verbal and vocal cues. Nothing pisses me off more than the obnoxious person who refuses to let go of a potential sale. This is so outdated and turns off more potential clients than it ever returns with success.

Think about it, most people dislike taking a cold sales call. It doesn't help that so many businesses mass target and cold call people who have no need or use for what they're having people make those calls for. Ever received a sales call from someone who wanted to sell your home when you'd sold it the year prior and were living in another city and/or state? How about getting a call at dinner from a security company that wanted to sell you a home private alarm system, yet you live in a large apartment complex?

Be sensitive and listen to the tone of voice of the person on the other end of the call, there is nothing wrong with exiting gracefully, quickly and with class. Conversely, if you're the one making the cold call, LET THE PERSON OFF THE PHONE when they're signaling, they're not interested. If you must keep someone on to clarify and push more to make your sale, you should consider revising your "pitch" to capture all benefits more efficiently. Don't be that guy, or gal who simply won't take "not interested" for an answer. Please don't.

> ## For every 'YES' on something, you'll get 25 'NOs'. But it's crazy how much that 'yes' gives you hope.
> —Andre Agassi

I dedicated the largest percentage of this book to cold calling. This wasn't my intention from the start, however as I got further into each chapter a flood of memories came over me. My mind took me back to the immense challenges and stress that those first few years so happily challenged me with daily. For the first 16 years in my sales career, I had essentially zero leads and cold calling was the primary (essentially only) way I connected with potential clients. Additionally, I was on a 100% commission. In my opinion, there is no more difficult sales job than having zero leads, relying 100% on cold calling in a relationship-based sales system, and being paid only after you've closed a sale to the account paid status ∎

13

Cold Calling Part Do – Practical Tips

Ok, let me go through some tips and two decades of muscle memory to help you with your cold calling. Make sure you take a moment before you start below and grab a cup of coffee or start fresh tomorrow before reading on. Cold calling sucks. What I'm going to present below will help you both professionally and emotionally. Although cold calling is dying, it's still a skill you'll need and is worthy of practice and attention. You never know when you'll meet someone for the first time and need to spring into action. Remember, cold calling for my purposes encapsulates your first call, meeting (in person or virtually), or organically meeting in an elevator where you're expressing who you are and what your product or service will do to make someone better.

Attitude. It's your first cold calling day and maybe you're a bit anxious. This is a perfectly normal emotional state in advance of all the numbers you're going to be calling. Don't just sit down and pick up the phone and start dialing. Don't. Do. This. First, check your mindset. Are you in a good mood? Are you energetic? If you can't say a definitive yes to both, it's NOT the right time to start cold calling.

People can hear your smile on the phone. You bet they can. You better believe that all of us can interpret someone's attitude on a telephone call. Your tone, pace, pitch, etc., all reveal something about you to your recipient and his/her impression of you instantaneously. Remember, 20-30% of all communication comes in the form of our vocal elements. So, make sure you SMILE when you dial. ☺

Have your hit list ready and available when you sit down. There should be dozens and dozens of targets that you want to call on your prepared list, or more. When you get those positive calls, they don't necessarily have to be someone agreeing to an appointment, sometimes they can be a friendly person telling you about a date in the future to call back. Any call that ends in a positive experience is the point. Take that positivity and parlay it into more calls.

Don't ever get up and walk away following a positive cold call. This is the moment when you have a small victory, and you want to use it! It's going to naturally amplify your vocal presence for your next call(s). This is the time when your voice, your confidence and your best will be on display from a telephone standpoint. Your vocal instrument is as warmed up and as red hot as it'll ever be. Don't let it go to waste! Bang out several more calls.

Once you've gotten two negative contacts/calls back-to-back, get up and walk away from your phone for at least 10 minutes. Get a coffee, go chat with a teammate, and try to laugh, meditate, or do anything other than allow the most recent two negative calls to remain on your mind. Don't sit around stewing and allow these negative calls to steal your positive, energetic mindset. Just as people can hear your smile on a cold call, they can also see your frown. ☹

Negativity works the exact same way that positivity does with your cold calling tone and energy. You cannot disguise your voice if you're down and dejected from getting kicked in the ass making back-to-back negative experience cold calls. Those who pick up your call will hear your mood. You may think that they can't. You may fool yourself into believing that you're of the same attitude and emotional state as you were right after the last good call, but I can assure you, you're not.

The smallest of things can tip off someone to your state of mind. Tone, pace, choice of words, all the vocal cues of communication. You think you're in command and displaying a positive professional demeanor, but you simply aren't at your best. You're being weighed down so why would you risk unintentionally sending a less than positive and totally energetic attitude on a cold call? After all, that call could be "the ONE!" No need to rush and slam in a few more calls when you're just not your best.

Learn to accept rejection. The reality is that you'll be rejected many more times than anyone wants or anticipates. Remember when I told you never to personalize a cold call rejection? Now's the time to dive into that. Here's my litany before I begin cold calling. I take a minute and I tell myself (well I think it, not talk to myself for fear that my coworkers will think I've lost my shit), whoever picks up the phone on the other end of the line may not be in the mood for this call and may be rude. They do NOT know me as a person at all. I'm a nameless, faceless individual who is simply interrupting their work at this moment. If they're rude and aggressive, just get off the call as quickly as possible and let them get on with their day. Don't get off the call with any feelings that you've failed, or that you suck at cold calls and sales, or anything else negative. The behavior exhibited by them is their issue and their emotional state of mind. Not yours. You're doing what you were hired to do, what you want and need to do, to get an appointment to sell your goods or service. Nothing more, nothing less.

Be empathetic. You never know the emotional state of the person who's going to pick up the phone until the moment they pick it up. There could be personal or professional stress that we can never know and they're simply reacting and responding to a very negative state they aren't able to control. If someone isn't nice, is aggressive, or rude on a cold call, show them empathy. The reality is that there are a thousand different things that could have set the person off prior to you getting them on the phone.

The best suggestion I have, should you find yourself unnecessarily taking fire from someone's emotional shotgun is to state, "I'm so sorry to bother you, it sounds as if something's not going well on your end, I hope you have a better day and I'm sorry for the interruption." This is your only chance at pulling off a miracle. If delivered in a warm, empathetic, respectful, and sincere tone, there is a chance (small, but still possible) they snap to and realize they have an empathetic stranger on the other end of the line who ac-knowledges things are tense. This quick and emotionally intelligent response has the possibility of changing the person's attitude instantly and thanking you for your understanding.

They can (again not often) but they can, continue and accept your call at this moment or ask you in a sudden change of attitude to call back tomorrow. This is a win for cold calling as now you and this person have this "moment" where they were unnecessarily stressed and giving you, their negative attitude and you displayed kindness. They recognized your understanding and consider-ation to let them go immediately and their brain automatically makes you a good guy or gal.

Get it? That's empathy folks. This quick, almost instantaneous, interpersonal moment on the phone is somewhat equivalent to certain times you may have witnessed or personally experienced in a friendship. Think back to a time when you had a conflict with someone that you didn't really know and the result was that you became not just friends, but good friends. Or, getting into a fight with someone who is a friend, but after the fight and reconciliation, the friendship became stronger. There is something within our mind that results in having an attraction and connection to someone if a negative incident ultimately ends positively. Oddly enough, the more significant the stressor or confrontation, the stronger the relationship becomes once it's corrected.

The potential customer or current customer is *not* always right. "The cus-tomer is always right." No. Nope. That's a nice, cute old phrase that worked at a very different time in our country's history. The increasingly abusive, confrontational, and flat-out disrespectful dialogues with potential targets and stressed-out buyers is sadly more frequent than ever before. Choose your moments wisely and, yes, I am a supporter of the occasional check yourself dialogue with rude prospects.

Negate and minimize any verbal or emotional abuse towards you and certainly to your inside sales team. Don't be weak. Stand up for yourself and your support team and make it clear quickly and firmly that you won't tolerate any disrespect.

The Bad Apple. Sometimes when you're cold calling you get a bad apple. There's absolutely nothing you can do or say to change this person on the call. It doesn't matter what the reason is or why, you simply can hear they're not in the mood at this moment and are ready to fight (verbally). These times are rare, but, if you should find yourself on the line with a bad apple, as I mentioned earlier, here is all you need to do: "I'm so sorry (insert their name if you have it or Sir/Miss will do), I apologize for the inconvenience allow me to let you go." Click. That's it. No more words need to be said. Quick, respectful, and simple. Exit gracefully before this bad apple can have a negative impact on your state of mind.

Be in the right frame and state of mind to smile and dial. Again, for emphasis, your energy, tone, and tempo all need to align and send the same message; that you are comfortable, confident, and competent to be making this call.

Have your cold call message memorized but be able to deliver it naturally. You immediately need to declare why you're calling. Never ever never allow the person picking up the phone to ask, "Why are you calling?" If they get that out before you tell them why you're calling, you're in the red zone. If they beat ya to it, this often means that they're not going to give you any amount of time other than to shut you down.

Be able to answer, "How are you different from your competitors?" flaw-lessly and with confidence and style. Bonus note: This is also one of the best questions you can ask from your side when interviewing for a new sales po-sition. If they can't answer it quickly, efficiently, and convincingly you're most likely in a mediocre company that's simply trying to throw more salespeople against the wall to see who sticks.

Timing is everything! Day of the week, time of day – put some thought into it. Jump in the shoes of those people you will be cold calling, assume they're less than happy to be taking the call and be creative and quick to the point. I have a formula that I've always used for the best days and times to cold call. I have no data to support this, just my personal reflections. The best days of the week are in the following order: Friday, Thursday, Wednesday, and Tuesday. Stop. Don't cold call on Mondays. Think about it. The best times to make cold calls on the aforementioned days are: 10:45 – 11:45 am and 3:45 – 4:45 pm. Why? Fridays are the last day of the work week and getting someone before they're getting ready for lunch or just about to leave for home on the last day of the week will give you the best chance to get them at their organically happiest days and times of the week. On a side note, I'll often reply when asked (on those rare occasions by a potential new client from a cold call) what works best for me with something like this, "Could we please schedule for whatever day and time of that day you're in the best mood?" This is a nice way to get a chuckle and more importantly they'll usually give you that day/time and that is what you want!

Personalize the voicemail message. If you can find anything out about them via LinkedIn or social media, use it. For example, if you notice someone attended San Diego State University, you begin by loudly proclaiming, "Go Aztecs!" before leaving a brief message to connect. This shows that you're aware this is the international shout out for all those who attended or support that university. How about if you notice something on the news or on the company's website about a recent success or big reveal? Begin with a sincere congratulations on what you saw or read as this can help connect. Or perhaps you discover that a client's new product or service is a perfect fit for your product or service. These are great ways to leave messages that will enable you to succinctly connect to your prospects.

Mention any referral you had or name-drop a relationship they may know. For example, leaving a message and telling the person that so and so referred you specifically to them for the purpose of…is a strong way to leave a message. Also, if you have a relationship or a friend of a friend inside that has weight, or is a shot caller, dropping this relationship is also a good way to get consideration for a callback.

Use cliffhanger or teaser messages. Maybe you leave a message that indicates you've recently helped (or dramatically improved) a company's product or service that is known within their industry. You could further reveal that you have "several" (note specific word choice here) ideas on how you could similarly do so for their company.

Be different. Try something new and refreshing. Perhaps after leaving a few messages attempt an accent. Leave a good (low risk of offending) joke, a startling statistic, an interesting life hack, or fun fact. Play with the messages and try to stimulate the person enough to want to call you back!

Leave short, creative voicemails. The primary key to leaving your best voicemails is to make them short and sweet. Be creative while getting to the point quickly. Don't try to be too cute as you risk the messages backfiring. If it feels too canned, or too disingenuous, most likely it is. You'll know when you've delivered the right voicemail as it will feel right and most likely yield a higher percentage of call backs. By the way, be clear and make sure not to forget when you're dazzling someone in 15 seconds that you don't eject from the call without leaving your contact information and call to action. Ouch!

No show is still a good go! If you schedule an appointment and your target forgets, don't fret. This provides an opportunity to display empathy for their schedule change, mistake, or absent mindedness. It doesn't hurt to alleviate their guilt by telling them you grabbed some coffee nearby and got some good work done. By and large when someone misses a meeting they've previously agreed to and scheduled, they'll feel a slight sense of obligation to rescheduling and ensuring their meeting with you. This gives you the opportunity to come into your first meeting with more confidence and more than likely a more attentive audience. This is a good way to begin a relationship by displaying empathy and ensuring the person that you're understanding and grateful they rescheduled ■

Hi, My Name Is...
Networking

The more hands you shake,
the more money you make.
—Brad Lee

Change your damn mind(set)! If you're like me and have, are, or plan to avoid networking "events," I strongly urge you to reconsider. My mindset for decades was to make fun of these types of things. Chamber of Commerce meetings, happy hours specifically for networking in your business community, or national conventions—shoot me please.

The irony of my dislike and avoidance of attending most things considered "networking events" (which I totally avoided the first ¾ of my career), is that I'm an extrovert, considered hyper social, and genuinely enjoy meeting new people. But put me in a fishbowl specifically surrounded by others there for business networking and I suddenly become allergic to people. I attend kicking and screaming. These types of events have always felt forced, contrived, and I've attributed an air of disingenuousness to these gatherings. I imagine walking up to a table, seeing the smiling faces of the wonderful people checking in attendees and my mind just thinks, "Uck! This is phony and awkward. What the hell am I doing here? I don't need these things. I meet people all the time and have no problem cold calling or approaching those I want or need to meet. This is forced and totally uncomfortable." Wrong, wrong, and if I wasn't clear, more wrong. Get over yourself. Yup, me too. If you have any sort of similar feelings towards networking events and you want to be successful in sales, it's time right here, right now to let them go. If my suggestion isn't enough, go to therapy, hypnotherapy, tapping, or do whatever you gotta do to get past this hang up as quickly as possible.

Networking is essential for a variety of reasons, but critical for expanding your network. See how that word just expands itself from noun (network) to verb (networking) so effortlessly. You need to do something to get something. It doesn't come on your good looks and charisma alone. Look at networking events in the following ways.

These events are an opportunity to meet new and interesting people. This same opportunity and possibility may lead you to connect with not only someone interesting, but also a person who can directly help your sales career. This person could help directly or indirectly (note the two-for-one here). Obviously, if you're targeting a specific client and the Director of Purchasing is in attendance, it's a no-brainer to approach them and give it a go. However, what if the director wasn't there but her neighbor was? Perhaps, her accountant or maybe a gal who is her daughter's dance instructor? Imagine you're just having an organic conversation with someone, they ask what you're doing there or what your goal was by attending the event and you slip out, "I was hoping to meet someone from XYZ company."

Immediately, this person replies, "That's bizarre. My neighbor is the COO for XYZ company, and we play cards almost every Thursday night." I'll let you take it from there, but I think ya get the point. I know these types of coincidences don't happen often, but they absolutely do happen. Know when they won't happen? When you don't show up! By not showing up, you miss out on life's magical ability to bring people together in ironic and coincidental ways. You know the lottery motto, if you don't play, you can't win. Well, if you don't go and show, you risk missing all the possibilities and probabilities of connecting with people you may want and need in your life.

In addition to improving the chance that you meet someone that could very well be helpful in your sales career, you also get the chance to market yourself by being there. Don't think that how you handle yourself, how you appear, speak, smile, dress and interact isn't being mentally downloaded to the other people in attendance. Maybe you gain nothing more than meeting some interesting people and making a friend or two. Or maybe you meet someone who knows someone (who knows someone) and neither of you two know that connection would very much help you, yet.

Let me address the frequently overlooked understanding of networking events. They're two-way streets. People often fail to remember that they're being approached or chatted up in someone else's hopes of expanding their network. We can get so focused on why we're there, what we're trying to accomplish, and who we're trying to meet, that we fail to connect dots in how we may help someone talking to us. Listening to who someone is and who they may know exclusively for your benefit minimizes the chance that you're open and listening to how you can help someone else. How great it would be if you met someone that can help you! Is it any less great if you don't meet anyone who can help you professionally, but you discover you can help someone else that you just met? If you've ever networked, met someone at an event or through networking and helped them, then you probably have experienced their sincere reciprocity, or at least continued efforts to return the favor.

The bigger the connection and help you give someone, the more they want to help you. The desire to reciprocate your effort and help you in return for a significant connection can last a lifetime. People can and will be forever grateful for introductions that are game changers, and they'll often remember you forever as being the reason, the person, or the catalyst that catapulted their career. Given the opportunity to return such an introduction they'll be ready to go the extra mile for as long as you're around. *As long as you're around.*

When you network and connect with someone, the goal should be to remain in a little bit of contact. This is where it can get challenging. I'm not suggesting everyone needs to be your best friend. Nor am I putting a cadence on how frequently you communicate. What I want to impress is that you do as much as you can to develop a sincere relationship, when you can. It could be a LinkedIn message on occasion, an e-mail, or text. The effort should be sustained and more than one and done. Ideally, you want to show the person that you're putting in effort without the immediate expectation or need for help. Again, networking and putting your best foot forward for the sole purpose of gaining something is a bit selfish, disingenuous, and restrictive. Preferably, you would want to display some sincerity that you're communicating to build a networking relationship. In essence, reach out for the sake of connecting, not just because you need something.

I connected with one young man through one of those employment agencies who represent folks looking for contacts to find their next job who said something very interesting on our first phone call. As he introduced himself, we immediately had a connection. You can pick up on someone's soft skills quickly from a conversation and he was sharp, humorous, engaged, and had phone charisma. He said, "J – I'm not necessarily looking for a job right now. I signed on with this career assistance company because I want to improve and expand my network. About three years back, I found myself without a job and absolutely couldn't find anything that remotely would pay me what I needed to make. I found myself in a very desperate place. I had no one to reach out to and my applications were simply being "ghosted" by human resources from a variety of companies. Fortunately, and by luck, I found a job a few months later. Those months prior to my new job I was devastated. I was tremendously depressed and in a low place in my life. After I began working the new job, I told myself that never again would I fail to actively and sincerely network. I never wanted to be in a position where I had no one to reach out to and no one in my network when I needed help. I made a commitment to do all I could to expand my network and meet anyone, anyplace, at any time that I could. I began reaching out to people on LinkedIn and as soon as I started to feel like the job wasn't all I was wanting, I contracted with X company to further amplify and increase my networking opportunities.

What he said next crystallized the power and meaning of networking. He essentially told me that a network (developed from networking) is something you should have because of continued relationship building and a conscious understanding that the more sincere of a network you have, the easier it is to ask for and receive help when you need it. It's not something you do when you need something immediately and are coming from a desperate place. He also stated that he allowed himself to become desperate and failed to actively network. His previous experience scared the shit outta him, and he never wanted to "911 network" again.

There's a difference between "911 networking" and attending events to expand your network. The point is that if you want to succeed in sales, you must be open minded to networking every day. This doesn't mean you're going to Chamber meetings weekly or conferences at the convention center quarterly, although there's nothing wrong with that. It means being open to meeting new people and maintaining some form of contact on occasion. Even a Facebook message for every birthday alert is better than nothing.

Work on your mindset and be open to networking. Realize it's a necessity to become the most successful salesperson you can be. Be prepared, willing, and comfortable speaking with people about what you do and who you are. Never forget you don't get a second chance to make a first impression. More importantly, don't forget that you can meet anyone at any time, and you simply never know where and when that most memorable or important meeting can take place. That person you're sitting next to on the subway may just be pretty important.

Practical Application

• **Use social media.** LinkedIn, Twitter, Instagram, TikTok, and even Facebook can serve as incredibly valuable resources for networking. These platforms offer unprecedented opportunities to connect directly with professionals in your field or areas of interest, allowing you to expand your network in ways that were previously unthinkable. Moreover, they provide a platform for sharing your accomplishments, endeavors, and involvement without coming across as overly self-promotional.

• **Attend various events.** Industry events, conferences, or trade shows are all great ways to meet new people and build your network. Of course, you want to keep these events relative to your industry and target customers. Come prepared with energy and focus on exactly what you want to achieve. Don't "wing it" and just show up hoping for networking to happen.

• **Be sincere and genuine.** Networking is about connecting with people that may be willing and able to help you, but you need to be open and looking for ways to help them! Be yourself; don't pretend and come off as someone you're not. If you want to be humorous, go for it and don't be afraid to let your personality shine through. Authenticity leads to likability, and this helps you in connecting and building strong relationships.

• **You F-up! Follow up that is.** Follow-up is crucial, so don't miss the opportunity! Whether you meet someone at an event or connect online, make sure to promptly and creatively reach out. Craft personalized messages that leave a lasting impression, promoting continued conversation and relationship growth. If you obtain someone's mobile number, light up that initial voice message with humor, fun, or genuine enthusiasm to inspire a response. Don't let a lack of reply discourage you from making another attempt. In my networking follow-ups, I typically adhere to a "two strikes and I'm out" approach. That's why it's important to initiate the follow-up immediately after meeting someone. Recall the iconic scene in the movie Swingers, where the guys debate the perfect amount of time to wait before calling a woman after getting her number at the bar? It's a classic scene. Avoid overthinking it – just act and reach out!

• **Volunteer.** Seek out volunteer opportunities that are related to your industry or field of work. Pick anything that you enjoy or believe in, and you'll expand your network. You'll meet like-minded folks and there's a nice bond between those that are involved in volunteer activities.

• **Get involved in a mentorship program.** By assisting others in their professional development, you establish connections with emerging talents and people entering your industry. This is a nice chance to share your expertise, skills and knowledge while developing meaningful relationships with newer and next generation members in your field.

• **Smile.** It's truly amazing how far a smile can take you in life. Smiling and displaying happiness sends a positive and powerful signal of charisma and makes you immediately of interest to others.

• **Use Carnegie's Rule of Three.** Using the person's name three times helps your brain remember their name. It signals that we've remembered their name from a split-second introduction and that they're memorable and we won't forget them. Be careful, too much of anything is just too much. Try to pull it off smoothly and sincerely. Ok?

• **Listen to others with sincere curiosity.** Be less actively trying to show how unique and charismatic you are and more actively interested in who they are and what they are saying (remember, it's very charismatic to actively listen). Give them your full attention by asking questions and displaying a sincere desire to get to know them and what they're interested in. I'm confident you'll see the benefit to this altered approach very quickly.

• **Discover someone's passion when having a conversation with them.** Everyone has a topic, sports team, or self-improvement that they love talking about. If you get it out of them and really listen (actively listen) while they're discussing it, they'll like you both consciously and subconsciously. Their brain will draw this conclusion because first you brought it out of them and second because they recognized how attentive you were while they spoke. If you hear something revealed during a conversation that is clearly important, for example, people or passions in their lives, find a way to remember this information. REMEMBER IT! Take those phone notes while that information is fresh on your soon to be stale mind.

• **Introduce yourself.** I know this one is shocking, and you didn't see it coming. Simply extending your hand and asking the other person's name is about the oldest, tried, and true way to break the ice there is.

• **Give a genuine compliment.** This can be as simple as complimenting something the other person is wearing or a recent accomplishment.

• **Talk about the event that you're networking at.** It's easy to ask what the other person thinks about the event, the speaker, or anything else that may stand out. Ask them what their goal was in attending, if they were looking to meet anyone in particular, etc. Just imagine if you happen to know someone in the industry, if not that exact person/role in a related industry.

• **Ask for advice, information, or help.** If you're sincerely interested in learning from the other person, ask for their advice on a topic or help if you're working on something in the same area. People LOVE to be helpful and connections form when asking for the simplest of help.

• **Share a story.** Share something that is either humorous or topical to the event itself or its purpose. People love stories.

• **Ask open-ended questions.** This sounds so simple, yet we fall into the same trap time and time again when asking professional and personal questions. Yes, no, yes, yes, no. If you pause and think about the question to ensure it's open ended, you'll go so much farther in your relationship building. Try writing down five to 10 open-ended questions that you feel comfortable using before heading out to any event. Practice them over and over. You'll quickly see how open-ended questions make conversations much easier and natural. Just remember, when listening (actively listening) and you want to question something you just heard, go for more open-ended questions so that the other person can continue, and the conversation just takes off ■

Impressing people is utterly different from being truly impressive.
—John Boyd

Build It...
They'll Come
Relationship
Building

If you believe a business is built on relationships,
make building them your business.

—Scott Stratten

Be genuine. Whenever given the chance, I've often believed (and lived) that displaying vulnerability demonstrates authenticity. Having the guts to display vulnerability is another tremendously powerful way to highlight your sincerity. People view those who aren't afraid to share vulnerabilities as genuine and trustworthy and these feelings lead to deeper relationships and more successful sales. If a significant portion of the country believes salespeople are dishonest, doesn't it make sense to try and exhibit behaviors that display the contrary?

Life offers many opportunities to show others that we're not too insecure, anxious, or affected by ourselves. However, far too many people stay far away from displaying any vulnerability and similarly would never think of making fun of themselves. I think we've somehow evolved into being, or continuously trying to be "cool" to the extreme and often at the expense of our emotional health. At some point along the way we stopped laughing at ourselves. Self-deprecation is a relationship building tool that is too infrequently used. I'm not suggesting that you use self-deprecation routinely. Too much of anything is too much and constant self-deprecation displays psychological insecurity among other things. No, use it at the right time and place to demonstrate that you can make fun of yourself, you aren't too arrogant, sensitive, or insecure, and that you can laugh out loud at your mistakes.

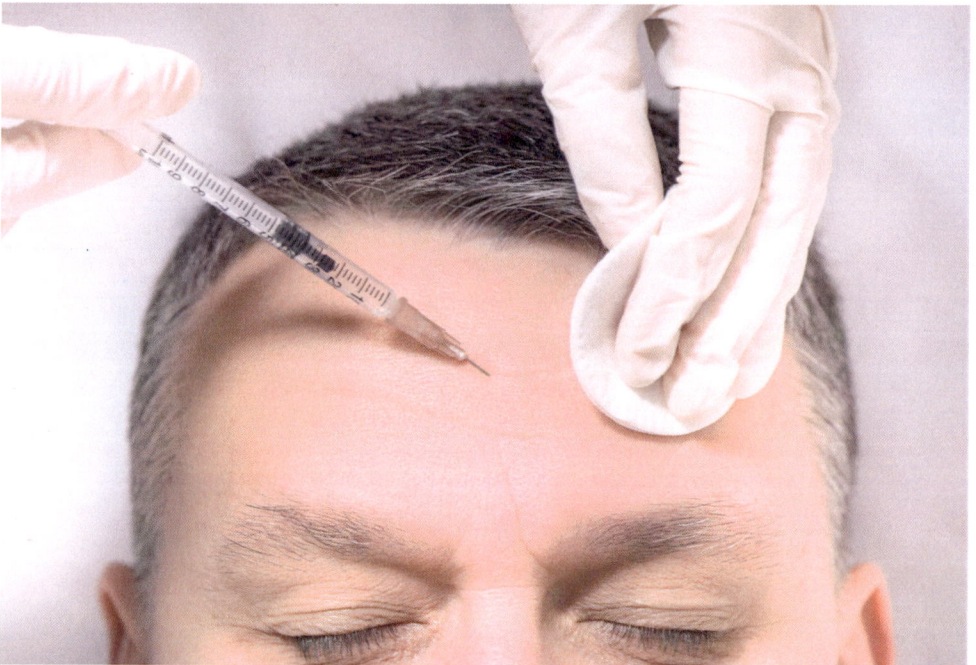

My wife is an RN. She'll tell you that she's not a "real nurse" as she immediately went to work for cosmetic surgeons in Southern California after receiving her Bachelor of Science in Nursing (BSN). Fast forward a couple of years into her career. She's developed a solid reputation for being hardworking and likable. There are some perks of working in this industry, such as discounted or occasionally free Botox, fillers, lipo, pretty much anything her specific doctor did in their office, for herself and her immediate family. Well, I made the decision one day to get Botox. Yeah, what the hell. I'm vain. I was aging hard (still am) and the price was right. I was ready to shave a decade off my facial clock. Ready, set, stick. Ok, that wasn't so bad. Fifteen minutes later I'm out the door and heading home.

Three days later I have a presentation on a new project for TaylorMade Golf. As I'm getting ready that morning, I notice that my forehead has frozen to such an extent that my already deep inset eyes have been pronounced and accentuated even more. I literally look insanely pissed off as my forehead (five-head) is now sloping straight down over my eyes. I can't use my muscles to pull back my skin. Immediately, I started to panic. I looked noticeably bad and strikingly mad. It's obvious I've had something artificial done to my face. It's not the same face that the receptionist nor three of the five marketing team members I've previously worked with will recognize. For the two poor bastards whom I've never met, I simply look like an intense, aggressive, and angry man. What can I do? I want the project; I need the project. I'm embarrassed like rarely before in my life and I can't hide it.

So, I begin the presentation with "I'd like to focus this meeting on what it would cost you not to utilize my re-design rather than what it would cost you to spend on re-designing…However, before I jump in, I want to discuss the 500-pound elephant in the room. (PAUSE) My forehead. Folks, there's no dancing around it, I had Botox for the first-time last week. It doesn't matter that my wife is a cosmetic surgical RN and I got it for free. What matters is that I can't have any of you believing I look like this normally. I'm not mad, upset and most certainly not feeling angry right now. What you're seeing is the frozen forehead effect of someone who didn't respond as well as he had hoped to free Botox." The reaction? Take a wild guess. Hysterics! Every single person was laughing. I delivered this story without missing a beat. I was dry, serious, matter of fact, and only had one choice. I had to expose my vanity and the subsequent price I paid for it. Self-deprecation gang, it rarely fails and truly helps build relationships and in case you're wondering, I absolutely got the project and made two new contacts within the marketing department.

> **Be authentic! Once you accept your flaws,
> no one can use them against you.**
> —George R.R. Martin

One time I was instructing a class of 12 students on how to deliver an exceptional presentation in Oklahoma City. As was typical, we began the class with some self-introductions. I requested that during their intro each student reveal a presentation topic that they wanted to use and build on throughout the course. There was one attendee who appeared to be about 70 years old. Following his 60 second introduction, two things were clear. First, he was the 11th or 12th out of 12 students in terms of comfort and delivery skill. Second, he loved his grandchildren; and they were a significant source of pride and importance to him. He stated that he would be presenting about his grandchildren. I pressed him to be a bit more specific. He struggled initially to articulate what he was going to say, however, with a little discussion we were able to help him dial it in. His final decision was that he would craft his presentation around the importance of leaving a legacy to his grandchildren.

The course spent most of the time drafting, practicing, and delivering the introduction section of a presentation. What this meant is that we would get to see the students come up and work on the same portion of their presentation several times throughout day one. Each time they would inevitably get better and more comfortable. On this gentleman's last rep of delivering the introduction section of his presentation something unique happened. When it was his turn, he came up and he had his PowerPoint on the screen. The image was a rainbow over a field somewhere in

Oklahoma City. He began discussing the rainbow as a metaphor for his topic, or at least this is what he appeared to be doing. Before he could make the connection between this rainbow and his grandchildren, he broke down crying. Not simply tears running down his face, but the sounds a man makes when he can't hold in the emotional pain any longer and loses the control that he's displayed most of his life. This lasted about 15 seconds before he began to compose himself. He took a moment and immediately went into the remainder of his presentation, finishing it strongly. Initially, I froze while observing this moment. I was so moved that I approached him and stood beside him in front of the class for a lengthy pause. I thanked him for having the courage to stand there and overcome such a powerful emotional experience. I looked at the class and asked them what they were feeling watching him. Most of the eyes looking up were somewhat watery and they replied in a variety of manners how powerful his display of total vulnerability was at this moment. How it locked them in to every word, sentence, and gesture he was making as he continued and plowed through his introduction.

I wouldn't suggest that you discuss any topic at length that is so emotional for you that you are unable to maintain a coherent overall presentation. However, I am most certainly encouraging you, should you ever be presenting or in a meeting and something topical arises that is emotional for you personally, not to hide it. In life and in business, it displays courage and instant relatability that few things can match.

This class experience was tremendously powerful and moving. I wanted to share it to illustrate that displaying vulnerability is not a bad thing nor a weakness. I understand why there's an outcry at present for men to be more "manly" and not show any feelings or emotions. However, don't equate an opportunity to show vulnerability, when connecting with someone, as a behavior that demonstrates weakness of character. People can relate to vulnerability, and because it's not often displayed, it's a super powerful way to connect with someone in a sales meeting, or any conversation to quickly earn trust. Someone willing to let their guard down with anyone new in their life is generally seen as someone who is sincere and genuine. It's a natural association to feel they're trustworthy as a result and this quickly begins the relationship developing process. Remember, most people are suspicious of salespeople's honesty and motives. Showing sincere vulnerability is a real and positive way to connect with someone during a sales presentation or when meeting someone. You'll leave a compelling and memorable impression and connect on a personal, relational level.

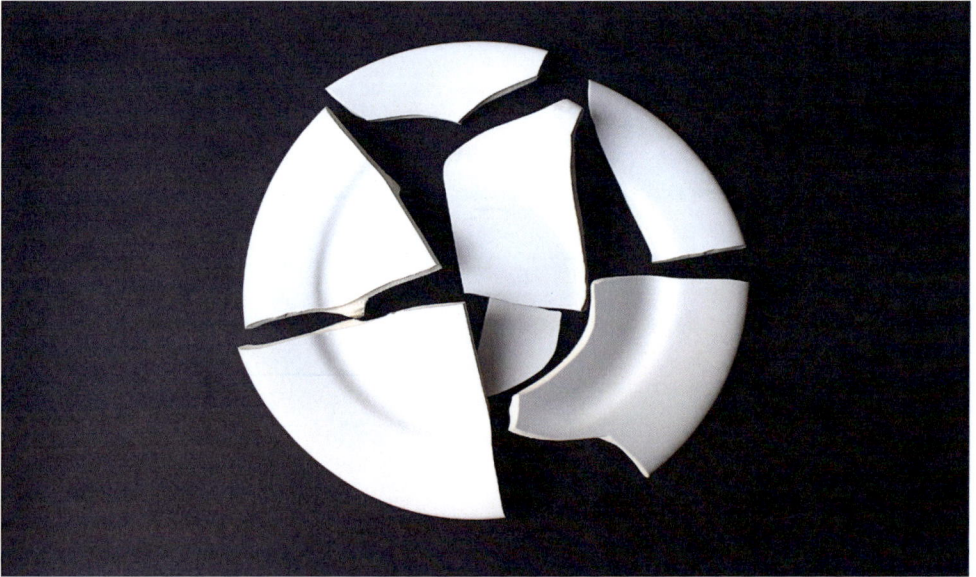

Real dishes break.
That's how we know they're real.
—Marty Rubin

If you are committed to developing a relationship with a business target, then it's always helpful to learn as much as you can about the individual and their company prior to engaging. Having an awareness and understanding of their situation is of great benefit. The more you can get to know about someone before meeting them, the more natural it is to begin to relate to who they are and what they are dealing with. On a personal level, combing over someone's LinkedIn account especially toward the bottom where more personal info is often shared such as hobbies, interests, or charitable work. On a professional level, understanding their role and responsibilities and acknowledging challenges, stresses, and other difficulties they deal with instantly connects us. The goal is to take a professional introduction or meeting, get to know someone, and then make it personal. Personal in the very best sense of the term. The person, NOT the professional. The real face behind the company's face.

Know that old line, "It's not personal, it's business." Even more common is the average manager who routinely goes to the "don't personalize" answer every time you look for guidance or simply need to rant after a tough day in the field. Successful salespeople absolutely have personal relationships with their clients and their business. They're not just intertwined; they're glued together through trust and time. This is exactly what I'm imploring you to take away from this book. If you want to increase your sales, it happens fastest and lasts the longest when you've developed a sincerely significant relationship. Relationships are personal!

The ability to develop a relationship sincerely and quickly is a soft skill that can't be emphasized strongly enough. Business IS personal, it's about personal relationships and connecting with those we trust and enjoy being around. You're going to know within 10 seconds to 30 minutes if an individual wanting to do business with you is someone you want to work with. The first 15 years of my sales career, I had only one differentiator, myself. Only one. My company was a packaging distributor, more of a broker, as we had only a few warehouses around the country and my office didn't even have that. As a company, we didn't do a single thing differently than anyone else in the packaging distribution space. In fact, we often had less to promote than our primary competitors. If you were to look up relationship-based sales, a simple photo of my company would have been the dictionary definition. We literally had no industry differentiators to offer.

Strong interpersonal relationship skills take a salesperson further than any differentiator a company can have, with perhaps one exception. Those companies that invent something of massive consumer significance and it's your proprietary good or service (one of kind thing). Recall what Gitomer said about all things being equal, people buy things from people they like. Also, all things being unequal, people still buy things from people they like. Strong relationship building skills increase your likability and trust. These things help draw others to you and naturally sales begin to take off. Focus on being authentic and building relationships so that when pricing comes up, you can speak comfortably rather than start playing verbal chess. I don't mean you may not face an objection after you've built a relationship with a prospect; I mean that your relationship building efforts and ability to communicate will guide the process and allow for an openness from your buyer that reveals all you need to know.

Be intentional and diligent when building relationships. Anything worth doing, well it's worth doing well. Don't half ass it, be creative and spend the energy in building relationships.

As I wrote this chapter, it reminded me of something that came up many years ago. I had been in my sales job about five years and my wife, and I were buying our first home, nothing short of a miracle in Southern California. I only had to drive 51 miles to get to my office each day to be able to afford it! But hey, I'm not salty. When it came time to unload the moving truck, I had five separate clients of mine at our new home in comfortable workout clothes ready to work. My customers took time out of their weekends to help my wife and I move into our first home. Perhaps you've heard of the saying if you really want to know who your true friends are, ask everyone you know to help you move. This will show you who the truest of them are. In addition, I had a few of my law enforcement friends rally that moving day as well. One of my cop friends pulled me aside and said, "Sully, these are your clients? You sell things to these guys? How in the hell did you get them out here to move your shit?" It didn't occur to me at that time as to "how or why" they came. However, as the years have gone by and I've become increasingly more certain that sincere relationships are the primary thing that matters in sales, and in life. I understand why they came out on a weekend all the way up to our new home in Temecula, CA. They were sacrificing their personal time just as any of us would for those we have a legitimate and genuine relationship with. I had earned their mutual respect through my effort, reliability, transparency, authenticity, listening, rapport building, and empathy. Thank you, fellas, once again, for moving those boxes and furniture with us. More importantly for the purchase orders, the laughs, the trust, and friendship. You made my work worthwhile on so many levels.

You can make more friends in two months by becoming interested in other people than you can in two years by trying to get other people interested in you.

—Dale Carnegie

What's the point of sharpening your soft skills? To improve your ability to develop significant, legitimate relationships both quickly and sincerely. I suggest that you spend twice as much time relationship building as you do working on a particular project for a new prospect. This way, should you lose the job, or aren't awarded the RFQ for any reason, you've developed the relationship. The relationship will provide you with another opportunity one day without having to go through all the energy required to get to that point in the first place. Take a run-down memory lane on that cold call and how many times it took to get that opportunity to develop that relationship. It sure is nice to not have to replicate that process, however that's exactly what you'll end up doing if you fail to build a relationship.

Build it and they will come...and stay!

A mistake I've observed too many times in my sales career is that my teammates would develop a relationship over the course of time and either lose their business within the company and stop communicating with their buyer or once their buyer left, failed to stay in contact with them. Here is where sincerity in relationship building and development is tantamount.

First, maintaining a business relationship when there is no more business displays a genuine effort in continuing the relationship. It says, no screams, "We've known each other for a while and I won't stop asking you to grab a bite or anything, just because you're not sending P.Os." Second, it enables you to approach the person much easier and with comfort when you do want to engage in new business at their new job, or after having lost the business for some time. Usually, if you legitimately maintain all your relationships, they'll come back to you when they're in a position and able to help your business. At worst you've gained a friend and potential contact for your future. At best, you've gained a friend and advocate with whom you'll regularly work with on improving your future. The point of the point? Know or learn how to make a real friend! What in the hell are ya waitin' for?

Most, if not all, opportunities in our lives come from other people. Improving your soft skills may be the most important focus one could have to increase the likelihood of greater opportunities. Think about this. Every one of us at some point interacts with someone else who is going to be making a or the decision on something, person, or event of great(est) importance in our lives. Why wouldn't we want to work on being the best version of ourselves? We spend billions (or more) as a country on personal physical improvements and cosmetically enhancing ourselves. Every single aspect of our faces, our bodies, our clothing, our scents, etc. We're completely homogenized when you think about it. Imagine putting in the dollars to improve our soft skills and that investment (work) translating into us being more charismatic, better communicators and active listeners. Maybe even more empathetic and continuously improving on our leadership abilities to list a few.

I hope that you'll consider this as you go forward with your lives. You can show up with the most freshly shaved, moisturized face, most expensive perfect haircut, smelling like $500 and wearing a suit or similar that is flawless both in design and tailored fit. However, if you lack strong soft skills, you risk losing the very opportunity you're physically preparing for, whatever that is! The final decisions made for us, about us and on us, arise overwhelmingly from our displayed soft skills, not our appearance. I'm not advocating that looking our best isn't important, only that it seems crystal clear to me that our priorities are out of balance. Perhaps our egos are yet again playing the great psychological defender when it comes time to consider spending money on improving things about us from a psychological or behavioral standpoint? Maybe it takes too much energy to work on our inner self versus the faster, more exciting outer self? Dunno, but I do think the next time you want to truly consider being your best, why not start from the inside (the most important side) out!

Practical Application

• **Be authentic.** Be unapologetically you.

• **Build a genuine relationship with your clients based on mutual trust and respect.** Don't play customer golf (meaning letting them win just to let them win). Get rid of the "tit for tat" mentality. It never works when you keep score in a relationship in business or in life.

• **Display empathy.** Put yourself in their shoes, especially when you see they "need tying."

• **Listen actively.** Show your give-a-fuck-ness and focus on what they're telling you. Understand their needs and concerns.

• **Respond.** Be prompt and show respect by reacting quickly to your clients' requests and priorities.

• **Be transparent.** Secrecy is rarely necessary and there is a clear difference between withholding information and sharing for the sake of sharing. Avoid hidden agendas as they'll quickly get you eliminated.

• **Build rapport with your clients.** Do this by showing interest in your clients' work, their hobbies, and passions; whatever is important to them, professionally and personally. This is how friendships are built over time.

• **Be reliable.** Strive to be your client's "go to" person. We all have one in our lives, the person we turn to first when we really need some information or some actual thing. Be dependable so that no matter what they ask or request, you're "on it." Speaking of the phrase, "I'm on it." Think about the times in your life when you've really needed something from someone, personally or professionally. When you text or call these people without hesitation they reply, "On it." or "I got you." No lengthy explanation as to why they can't or how challenging your ask is going to be on them, just simply, "Consider it done." The sense of relief we feel is massive. This only needs to happen a few times at the earliest stage of developing a relationship and you'll elevate incredibly quickly in someone's personal and professional life. Be the one person that handles it quickly without expecting things in return. This is relationship building gold.

• **No one-way streets.** Relationships develop and grow when BOTH people share information. Not just professionally, but personally ■

16

If You're Leading...
Check Who's
Following: Leadership

I define a leader as anyone who takes
responsibility for finding the potential in people
and processes, and who has the courage
to develop that potential.

—Brene Brown

Understanding the distinction between a boss and a leader has been explained and discussed for a long time, and it's widely acknowledged that being a leader is far superior. Within this chapter I'm striving to provide insights and guidance specifically tailored to future or current sales leaders. While numerous books delve into the subject, I'm simply highlighting some key points. I'll outline what you absolutely should and shouldn't do if you aspire to become a successful, impactful, respected, and admired leader. After all, why settle for anything less? If you find yourself with any justification for wanting anything other than that, perhaps being the "leader" isn't the right course for you.

Have you ever been a leader? How about a sales leader? Any leader at any job? Admittedly, from the minute I had my first professional job, I felt in my bones that I had the natural talent and ability to be a better supervisor, manager, boss (whatever title), than the person in charge of me at that time. From day one. Most of my life I had felt that way right up until my very first leadership role. I was flat out wrong. Talk about a cold bucket of water right in my face. Worse still, it wasn't until I was 43 that I had my first real sales leadership role, and I couldn't use immaturity or youth as an excuse.

It was everything I didn't know (and couldn't possibly know) without walking in a leader's shoes. I was determined to never be a "boss," but a true leader, based on the very best definition. What I failed to recognize was that there's much more to do in a leadership role and the tremendous responsibility if – IF – someone wants to be a valued, trusted, and a respected leader.
Not a boss, anyone can take that title and role. The true goal for any leader is to be sincerely respected for how you interact with people and what you give to those under your direction, not simply your knowledge in the industry. Leaders are valued for how they treat people, how they empathize with people all while maintaining accountability across the board. This is the area I fumbled in more than once. I had the interpersonal skills, the energy, the sincerity, the willingness to lead by example, the empathy, the dedication, more than enough knowledge, but what I didn't have (mostly) was the ability to balance a legitimate relationship of trust and care, as well as hold my team accountable when they needed it most.

Before you're a leader, success is all about growing yourself. When you become a leader, success is all about growing others.
—Jack Welch

Last year while I was facilitating a course on how to give an effective presentation, I had a unique opportunity to interact with an exceptional leader. Upon my arrival, this individual notified me that he would be attending the course alongside his team. First, this in and of itself is unusual. The leaders, management, bosses whatever word we choose, generally send their teams, and don't put themselves in this course. It's designed to improve public speaking and leaders often avoid it knowing they'll be standing and delivering video-taped presentations to be evaluated in front of their subordinates. As you can imagine, they are usually "busy" when the courses are scheduled. This gentleman immediately intrigued me when he said that he would be a participant during our two-day course. He stated that he not only wanted to improve, but also felt his team would benefit from observing him engage, interact, and demonstrate that he, too, had room for improvement, as well as having some real anxiety when presenting (vulnerability!).

Then he told me that there was a dark cloud over the two-day training as the company announced impending layoffs. He added that several folks in the class were candidates for layoffs and they were simply waiting for the announcement to see if they would make the cut. Layoffs were understood to be happening in the next week or two. He added that there was a general anxiety within the team and that he not only wanted me to know this, but to further ensure I took caution if someone appeared a bit more anxious than usual. I, of course, was grateful for the heads up and confirmed I understood and would be monitoring closely.

The class kicked off and I anticipated some hesitancy and less than enthusiastic participation. Much to my surprise and delight, they all came in ready and focused. At the end of day one, the leader asked me if I would meet him in his office for five minutes. We went inside his office, he closed the door, and this is where I had the remarkable opportunity to witness what has been one of the single greatest displays of leadership I've ever seen. He thanked me for coming in and I could instantly sense that he was in a different mindset. He was slightly dejected, depressed, and you could see sadness in his eyes. He said, "Jason, I just was notified of who is being laid off in our class and the announcement will be made at 9:30 tomorrow morning. Would you please break us for 30 minutes and we'll pick it right back up after?" "Of course," I agreed.

I was not going to inquire as to who the individuals were, but he volunteered to share them with me. As I look back, I believe he chose to share as he, the class, and I had created a bond (yep, the solid foundational beginning of a relationship) throughout the day. Additionally, I know he wanted to ensure that I had the heads up to be sensitive in case any of the three (out of 10) individuals displayed more anxiety or stress than the previous training day. He revealed two of the younger participants and one older gentleman were to be laid off. I paused and felt the weight of his feelings about the situation. For a moment, I saw his eyes welling up, but he remained stoic for the entirety of the meeting. The way he spoke, the cadence, the empathy, the humanity, and the vulnerability were so impactful and signaled such genuine sincerity from a leader, that I would be forever impacted.

As I write this story and try to convey the magnitude of this moment, it feels like I've let myself, you, and that moment down. I knew I'd use this story and was eager to share it, however, as I review it, it somehow feels lighter than I wanted. As he paused and I hesitated, he added that upon receiving the names, he had immediately gotten on the phone and had opportunities available for the two younger teammates to take another role within the company if they chose. It would be a lesser role; however, it would avoid them being laid off and keep them within the company and allow them to be in the best spot to promote down the road. He noted that they both had young families, and it had made him sick to consider not providing them with some option, some hope that he could stabilize a rather unfortunate and unpleasant announcement. He went on to say that the older gentleman, he would be able to "convince" to retire instead of having to lay him off. The manner with which he delivered the line "I'll convince him" was so powerfully persuasive that it made me curious enough to want to be there when they spoke.

The look on his face as he talked through the steps he took to go above and beyond for these three people that worked for him was so sincere, so focused, and so considerate that it's frozen in my memory. I had the opportunity to witness and appreciate his unwavering commitment and loyalty to the well-being of his team as well as his extraordinary example of leadership strength. I expressed my admiration to him, and he graciously acknowledged my words and replied, "How could anyone do it any other way?"

He then told me that he was promoted on the very same call and would need to relocate to another state for this advancement (one that was very significant). He was conflicted with emotion and although he had known he was under consideration; he simply couldn't enjoy it under the circumstances. He mentioned that the new ownership group, which was a massive global company, gave him the directives via a group Zoom call. He related that it was a cold delivery and that he quickly realized he would be leaving a position and a team that he felt very proud of to go enter a much more sterile role and surrounding group of people. He knew that his ability to have that type of impact and connection to a team may very well be coming to an end.

I felt compelled to tell him at that moment (knowing I was relatively insignificant in his life but feeling strongly) that what I had witnessed of his leadership and character was something that I hoped he never lost, no matter how high he ascended. He thanked me very sincerely and the last thing I said to him was that I understood the three wouldn't be coming back after the 30-minute break to hear the news. He replied, "No, I expect they'll come back and finish off the class." I was taken aback by his matter-of-fact delivery. I was looking at their possible reaction through my own emotional lens. No way would I want, nor have the focus, to participate in a training course on public speaking and present for the next seven hours knowing I had just been laid off, even with the boss's contingencies. Not that I would have stormed off, but I simply would've let management know I'd be returning home to be with my wife. Nope, not his team. I was a little skeptical, but so impressed by him that I knew if he felt this way, he must be right. Without missing a minute, true to his word, they all came back, participated, and gave it their all.

What an incredible experience it was to see firsthand all the way around. It gave me affirmation that there are still incredible people and leaders out there. I'll forever be grateful and mindful of what I observed. The empathy and subsequent action taken to minimize the impact on all three employees is the type of example that pushed me to write this book.

I once read someplace that leadership is a matter of the heart. The author was making the point that while results were critical for managing a business, the very best leaders balanced results with relationships – great relationships. No great leader ever succeeded by results alone. Let's apply this to that age-old leadership dilemma: is it better to be loved or feared as a leader? If you're loved, your team, your staff, your players, will perform, do, work, and even extend their days if you're around or not. If your people are afraid of you in terms of the consequences for not performing or doing what is expected, this too will produce certain outcomes. However, a team that has an opportunity to NOT do something asked of them by the person they fear, rather than love, confidently knowing there will be no way they are found out or face any consequences – they'll make the decision to give the least effort possible without facing backlash from the feared leaders request or desired goals.

I had a mentor tell me that too many leaders used their meetings to focus on improving negatives. He added that humans weren't wired to continually focus on negatives. He insisted that rather than focus on negatives routinely, focus on the positives within a team by asking people what was working well, how they got there, what they did, etc. This way, the team could see and hear what "good" looked like. Accentuating the positive versus revolving around the negatives. Highlighting and working on the positive things is something I've observed far too few times with previous leaders. The default playbook is to address the negatives and corrective actions. Try discussing the positives once in your next sales meeting and build off of them for the group. See if you can see and feel any differences.

Leaders are responsible for a company's culture. Whether they want to own it or not; it's implicit in their role and responsibilities. If you've purchased this book, my bet is you're going to be a leader at some point in your future profession or within whatever organization you're involved. Even if you fail to practice improving your soft skills, the very act of reading this book shows that you, at the very least, understand the importance of demonstrating soft skills. This demonstrates your emotional intelligence, and I bet you'll get to a leadership role one day. When you do, don't forget to own your role and all that it comes with. Don't accept the responsibility if you can't recognize that becoming the "boss" isn't a step down in workload, not if you want to be a real leader. Promoting within your organization to be a real leader doesn't mean your work life will get easier. It's quite the opposite. I saw a video clip of Simon Sinek saying that when you become the boss, you put yourself at risk to look out for others. This becomes one of your primary responsibilities. You don't do less work as you become more senior and ascend into leadership, you do more work!

We are at our most powerful moment when we no longer need to be powerful.
—Eric Michael Leventhal

Practical Application

- **Set a clear vision for yourself and your sales team.** Lead by example in such a way that your clients and team are inspired and motivated.

- **Communicate effectively and regularly with your client(s) and your team.** Schedule business reviews with your clients and regular meetings with your team to provide feedback, guidance, and any support they may need.

- **Assertively build relationships with your clients and team.** This displays a confidence and energy that is positively contagious. Positivity begets more positivity, and your clients and team will want more of you in the very best of ways.

- **Be flexible, adaptable, and willing to change for your clients' needs and those of your sales team.** Never stick to something that isn't working simply because "you've always done it that way." Being called rigid and stubborn isn't something to be proud of.

- **Strive to be innovative for your clients and team.** Even if there's nothing substantial, never stop seeking and experimenting with new, better, more efficient, or creative ways to do things. The effort will be noticed and have a very positive impact upon your clients, as well as your sales team.

- **Hold yourself accountable to your clients and team.** Service your clients positively, proactively, and consistently. In their service. If you don't want to be in the service industry, the sales profession isn't for you ∎

17

The End That Leads to the Beginning

Without the ability to end things, people stay stuck, never becoming who they are meant to be, never accomplishing all that their talents and abilities should afford them.

—Henry Cloud

We love to "rank" things. Whether it's our preferred Netflix series, favorite film, or album, we're always eager to hear what others consider to be "the best." We're captivated by people's responses to these "favorite" questions and eagerly anticipate their answers, either sitting front and center fully attentive or pretending to be occupied while secretly hoping to hear their reply. However, when it's our turn to provide our own top picks, we often freeze and stumble, unprepared to commit to a definitive number one. Nevertheless, we encounter these types of ranking questions and lists every day and enjoy the discussions and debates that follow. Ultimately, the truth is that ranking things is fun, and it brings people together whether we agree or disagree on who or what is #1.

I initially started out with the intent to rank the soft skills in their order of importance. Which skill was my #1 and absolutely needed to be practiced and so on down the line. Then, I hesitated. I concluded that soft skills are more interdependent than independent of each other. I tried several times to "rank" them and provide my top order. However, the more I listed several of the most necessary soft skills, the more I stumbled and couldn't bring myself to try and declare which was the best and most needed. The truth is, there are numerous soft skills and all of them are important. Sure, you can be deficient in some and more proficient in others, however, the person who works on improving all their soft skills will ultimately be the most successful salesperson. Further, he or she will be internally happy and externally admired.

In my 22-year sales career, I've laughed, I've cried, I've got into arguments with clients, and expressed every other emotion you can think of at one time or another. I shared my stories and weaknesses to highlight how deficient I've been in hard skills and how difficult I've made it on myself as a result. Yet, I overcame these challenges time and time again because of my soft skills. I took the WRONG way and the LONG way so frequently that there's NO way I should have made it in sales. No way. If not for the soft skills I possessed and realized were carrying me, I would've dropped out or been dropped by my second year in the profession.

My soft skills beat the hardest of challenges. In a world that is constantly telling us we need to be hard; you can take that step by being softer in your skill set.

I strived to demonstrate throughout this book that displaying soft skills sincerely and consistently aren't the only things you'll need, but rather the most important skills you'll need to be a successful salesperson. Skills by their definition mean that they can be learned. If you recognize you aren't all you can be in any of the areas I touched upon, why not work at it? I promise you'll improve in all areas of your professional and personal life! If you work at improving your soft skills, it's that elusive win-win we search for overall. You'll not only enjoy the benefit of being a better salesperson, but a better person. If your sales career doesn't go as hoped, your new and improved soft skills are going to powerfully propel you forward against your competition in any career. I hope that you've gained something from this book. Moreover, I hope that if you've been inspired or energized on any level, that you don't delay another day. Start actively working on your plan to improve your soft skills the moment you put this book down or swipe your last e-page. Don't let anything get in your way or distract you. Don't put it off and tell yourself you'll start tomorrow. You have the choice of a day one- or one-day response for improvement. At this very moment, grab a pen, make a note, or do any damn thing you can right now to take the first step to improving yourself. There's no wrong way, there's just a moment to begin change or risk allowing your momentum to evaporate and become less important as life gets in the way. Remember, BIG results can happen from the smallest of changes.

One inch of movement will take you closer to your goals than a mile of intention.
—Steve Maraboli

As I approached the conclusion of this book, I found myself reflecting on the initial motivations that drove me to write it. Surprisingly, I realize that my original reasons were not the sole driving force behind this endeavor. I unintentionally overlooked a significant factor that drove me to sit down and finally knock this out. Over the months of constructing this book, I began to become afraid. Afraid that my biggest strengths have always been soft skills and that they may be dying out because of technology and the newer generations' reliance on it.

While I believe that most folks from my generation understand the necessity and significance of having a command of soft skills, I have concerns about whether the younger, more recent generations truly comprehend or appreciate their value. It's come to my attention that many high school students nowadays express their romantic interests and plans for events like prom primarily through text messages. This sure made me feel old and out of touch. This reliance on technology for nearly every aspect of communication is quite startling to those of us who grew up in a time when such technology wasn't available or when it was certainly not relied upon as the primary way of communicating. I don't want to come off as one of those older guys who's pissed because he's not technologically keeping up. While this is true, I'm really concerned from my perspective that human contact, the element of human interaction, is being quickly minimized and diminished. If my soft skills aren't needed, aren't valued, or aren't a differentiator, I've got nothing of significant value for an employer. Now that may read a little dramatic, but it's literally accurate. Not only true, it's scary as I'm at a time in my life where I'm older, but still have a way to go in the workplace. As I watch technology, including artificial intelligence, develop I find myself increasingly concerned I'll be replaced by someone (or something) at half my salary. If technology is replacing soft skills, it's no longer about salary or age; it's simply about no longer needing the only tools I've ever possessed and used successfully. Is evolution phasing out what has always been my strength in the workplace? Are my soft skill advantages increasingly becoming less necessary?

I walked away for a couple days after writing the last paragraph. Some due to writer's block, but mostly to think about the near future and what I realized was concerning and causing me anxiety. Fortunately, after some time away and really thinking about the anxiety I've been experiencing, I've come to a positive outlook. The younger generations may be utilizing technology to communicate their thoughts and feelings more than ever. They may be normalizing communication via text and computer in ways we never thought would be possible or acceptable. As a result, their soft skills become much less needed or valued over time. We're seeing this daily in the workplace between the different generations who misunderstand each other due to their communication differences. There's a palpable frustration in many workplaces between those who utilize and rely on technology for communicating versus those who are more traditional and prefer to speak via phone or in person. As we start to subtract the most important elements of communication (body language, tone, inflection, etc.) we not only invite misunderstanding to counter-productive levels, but also, we depersonalize relationships by a lack of traditional interaction. There's still nothing for the foreseeable future that can replace seeing, touching, feeling, etc. between humans in the workplace.

Slowly but surely my concerns were redirected by my convictions regarding the importance of soft skills. I kept thinking about what's occurring and what we're rapidly losing. Then I reminded myself how oftentimes change comes after learning from our mistakes. We must learn from the past and recognize the unintended consequences of too much technology. I stopped and took some time to think about the newer generations and their experiences and understanding of the world. I understand that for those preferring to communicate behind a device, it's almost all they've ever known, so holding them to some negative or personal accountability is my ego trying to protect my future, emotionally or physically.

I now acknowledge that while technology and automation will continue to play an increasingly important role in sales, it is the personal attributes, the soft skills of salespeople that will ultimately determine their success. Witnessing and living through this change has been turbulent and stressful for me, as it has for many. I tell myself that we're in the middle of this new clash and time will reveal that human interaction and all the related soft skills will one day soon be our primary focus once again. After all, most communication both sent and received occurs via body language and vocal elements, so how could we survive behind a keyboard? As the light grows dim and technology continues to advance and depreciate soft skills, I remind myself that it's always darkest before the dawn. Remember, when it comes to sales and life skills, the softest are the hardest and absolutely the best!

– JS 🍀

People may not remember exactly what you did, or what you said, but they will ALWAYS remember how you made them FEEL.

—Maya Angelou

Dear Readers,

"I'm thrilled to have the opportunity to address you directly as a first-time author. Writing this book has been a labor of absolute love and I sincerely hope you enjoyed it. As a novice author, I understand your time is valuable, and I'm deeply grateful that you chose to invest some of it reading my work. If you've found the book engaging, educational, or helpful in any way, I kindly ask that you please consider leaving a review. Your words can make a significant difference, not just in the success of the book, but also in my motivation to continue writing and improving. Thank you very much for being part of this exciting new chapter in my life as a writer."

– JS

"May your coffee be strong and your Monday short!"

~ Irish Blessing

Acknowledgements

No book can be written without a tremendous amount of gratitude for several people. This was my first foray into writing (start date: 12/9/22, finish date: 12/31/23), and I can say with certainty, it's nothing short of work! Authors pour their hearts into their writing as you would expect. To write is one thing, to write something longer than an average high school paper while maintaining rhythm and adhering to some semblance of order is entirely another. It took me longer than I'll ever admit bringing this book to life. It was a tremendous learning experience and worth every hour spent. Nothing has made me feel as personally exposed as pressing send on the final manuscript for publication. There is no way I would have been here without the following people who deserve so much more of my thanks than any number of words can describe. To the woman that I met at Falls Lounge in Dearborn, Michigan who said "I do" 23 years ago. Since our first date, Jeanette's never failed to support me in anything I've asked. She's been unwavering in her love and is selfless when it comes to me and our family.

To my sons, Hudson and Lochlan, who allowed me to miss a significant amount of family time (for a long time), who at their ages only understand that "Dad is in the office working on a special project." Always know I could hear you both playing, laughing, and growing as I pushed forward to make sure I didn't quit. I hope one day you'll be able to read this and connect your memories to all those times I was in the office.

I have an entirely new perspective and respect for editors. To ask someone who has absolutely zero connection to your work, to care enough to methodically walk through every word on every page is simply impressive. To my editor, Dr. Lily Bruckner—I thank you eternally for putting up with the highest of maintenance. I threw a bucket of spaghetti on the wall for you, and you took each individual strand, placed them side by side and laid them all out together, in order. If not for you, this dream of mine would have remained just that. Putting all your passion, thoughts, emotions, and ideas (literally) into a stranger's lap and saying, "make sure it's readable and flows and doesn't make me look too bad" is a challenging ask of and for anyone. I owe ya one! No, I owe ya LOTS of ones.

To my dear friend who wore five + hats for this book, Donna KaDell (cover art, format and layout, graphic design, and rant recipient). You took the words and added images and final physical structure to bring this thing to completion. Thank you for sticking by my side and putting your heart into my project.

To New Year Publishing's, Dave Morris. Eternally grateful for the hand holding and sobering reality checks throughout this process. I'm so glad it was you. Go Aztecs!

To Barbara and Tom Latra, resting in peace. I hope you both are proud of what I've been able to accomplish. Your love and support remain with me forever and I miss you both.

To my mother and sister for cheering me on under stressful professional times I simply say: We've come a long way baby! I've never known a time without your love, support, and encouragement. How lucky I was to be born into our family. I love you both so much.

To my friends from Michigan to California and everywhere in between for telling me to keep pushing - great lookin' out!

To each of you who have bought this book, thank you for giving me the chance to help in any way possible. I sincerely hope you enjoyed it and can take away something that will benefit your professional and personal life.

Finally, to my stepfather, Peter "Pierre" Cousins, reading from Heaven. Pierre, I watched you through my adolescent eyes work relentlessly night after night in the small bedroom which became your office at 3437 Pardee. You taught me how to type on a computer and generously showed interest in my academics, in addition to regularly helping me with my schoolwork. You were an example of the absolute best in academia and one of the last of the Mohicans of scholarly gentlemen. Light your pipe and turn every page, knowing I thought of you with each one I wrote.

With the greatest of sincerity and gratitude,

Jason Sullivan

December 2023

The bad news is time flies.
The good news is that you're the pilot.

– Michael Altshuler

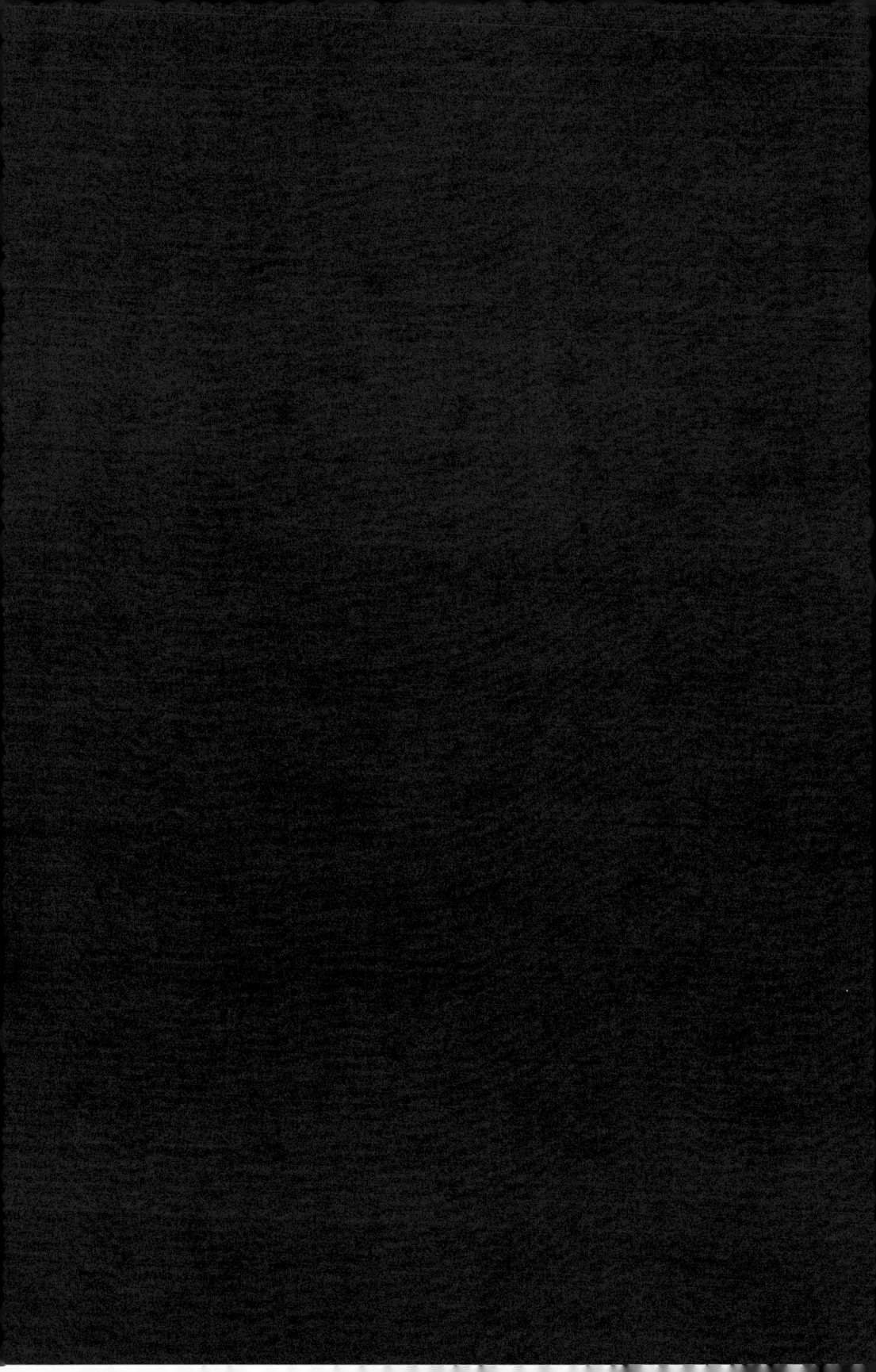

www.ingramcontent.com/pod-product-compliance
Lightning Source LLC
Chambersburg PA
CBRC090248230326
41458CB00114B/6530/J